FOREST LUNGS

A Poem

ANDREW G. ZUBINAS

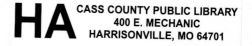

Order this book online at www.trafford.com
or email orders@trafford.com

Most Trafford titles are also available at major online book retailers.

Print information available on the last page.

ISBN: 978-1-4907-7406-0 (sc)
ISBN: 978-1-4907-7407-7 (e)

Library of Congress Control Number: 2016908760

Trafford rev.   06/17/2016

www.trafford.com
North America & international
toll-free: 1 888 232 4444 (USA & Canada)
fax: 812 355 4082

Touch, the winds of the forest.
Hear, the winds of the forest.

Lungs of the earth; the still, motionless forest breathes.
Lungs of the earth; spring tides of sunlight, autumn tides of sunlight.

Moss, lichen, mushrooms branching on a bronchus hollow log, split log.
Moss, lichen, mushrooms branching on a lobe of shady stone, split stone.

Rhythm, side-to-side sway movement of the tops of trees.
Rhythm, side-to-side sway movement of the cilia of trees.

Storm front in paddle movement, mirrors of the flashing undersides of silver leaves.
Storm front in paddle movement, murmurs of rustling, crackling, shaking leaves.

Dome, vault, canopy of leaves; tan antlers of a stag.
Dome, vault, canopy of leaves; white tail of a doe.

The stem of a flower; grooved bark, rough bark, brown bark, black bark, gutter bark.
The stem of a clover; furrowed bark, ridged bark, rutted bark, channeled bark.

Sprouting, growing plants protruding toward blankets of warm, dry sunlight.
Sprouting, growing plants protruding away from carpets of cool, damp soil.

Snapped bronchiole of elm, willow, maple, ash, oak, birch, and evergreen.
Snapped bronchiole flesh of twig, stick, branch, club, spike, and stem.

Stump indentation; the lobe of a pine, fine needle bed.

Stump indentation; the lobe of a poplar, veined leaf bed.

Many spaces in between the many low-voltage leaves, green leaves.

Many shades of green, mildly glowing sunlit fluorescent green, dark speckled leaflet green.

On the ground there are decaying brown leaves, dry leaves, moist leaves, soiled leaves.

On the ground there are scattered branches, pieces of wood, brown wood, rotting wood.

Forest fire, fire of cancer, honeycomb beehive inflamed, stingers modulated and guarded.

Forest fire, fire of emphysema, termite-riddled holes, beaks of woodpeckers in slow recovery.

Honey dewdrop woodland tears; post-rain crying, productive forest cough, forest sneeze, forest sniffle.

Honey dewdrop woodland tears; sweet sugar syrup of maples, amber-entombed insect.

Forest pleura raiment; oblique thread of vine and ivy, button of shrub and bush, hood of fern.

Forest pleura raiment; tundra cloaks, hardwood furs, deciduous pelts, rainforest skins, felt and velvet.

The woodland wheezes, the tree fell crackles, creaks with a "timber" gasp.

The woodland wheezes, cicadas ring loud, humming, murmuring a long winding down auditory haze.

Sylvan pulse of seasons; white and brown time, brown and green time.

Sylvan pulse of seasons; hours of red, orange, green, yellow, brown, and maroon—shortness of breath.

The forest breath of four seasons, time tattooed on the inked ring of a tree's torso; thorax of trees.

The forest breath of four seasons, rebirth inhaled and exhaled repetitively; thorax of trees.

Silent bellows of a forest voice; thoughts, roads, and paths of a song branching from a trunk.

Silent bellows of a forest choir; mountainside, riverside, brookside, valley, and vale of life's composition.

Forest, thick and dense, wild and untamed, green irises of nature.

Forest, thick and dense, wild and untamed, brown hands of nature.

Forest factory of elements tugged and hauled by a mesh of roots, each stitched into a capillary quilt.

Forest factory of elements warmed and cooled by summer fevers and winter chills—forest purges.

Rich forest; coins of frond, needle, awl, scale, stipule, petiole, lamina, microphyll, and sheath.

Rich forest; shapes of points, blades, hearts, triangles, ovals, sickles, teardrops, eggs, and arrowheads.

Forest sac, gathered harvest of the forest; sacs of pollen, sacs of nuts, sacs of wild blueberries.

Forest sac, gathered harvest of the forest; pristine clean air from the belly of a landscape.

Sac of woodland, belly beehive of honey, yellow honey.

Sac of woodland, bloodsucking mosquito belly of blood, red blood.

Arbor embolism; seed by wind, seed by water, seed by animal; simple.

Arbor embolism; seedling germinating bower, seed pod dominion; simple.

Treetop bristles; green puffs, green fog, green smoke, green clouds, green spot, dapple green.

Treetop bristles; red puffs, violet fog, maroon smoke, orange clouds, green spot, dapple green.

Acorn lung bud, rough crowned cartilage cap, smooth wooden cheek of a faceless knob.

Acorn lung bud, open doorway's pouch of dirt, unborn sapling womb of soil.

Strands of trees; nature's green harpsichord plucked by the brisk digits of a breeze.

Strands of trees; nature's brown violin notes rising, falling, and changing color.

Forest beam flu; rainy ice storm remnants glistening, melting, thawing in the sunbeams.

Forest beam flu; flocks of birds settling, perching, chirping, flying, fleeing in the sunbeams.

Lips of forest, mouth of forest; stoma of forest leaf.

Lips of forest, mouth of forest; stoma of forest clearing.

Rib of flood, rib of drought; fused tree histories of ring growths; rib of Eden.

Rib of flood, rib of drought; trachea tree of ring growths; rib of Eden.

Unsweetened soul of sapling seed leaves; shrine vital breath of Eden, garden prayers amidst olives.

Unsweetened soul of sapling seed leaves; forest shoots of gods, spirits, and sprites.

Forest broncholith, mountain forest boulder, dynamic traumatic forest blast lung.
Forest broncholith, mountain forest ball, rock and plant tension.

Diaphragmatic lake on the forest shore, oceans of muscle nourishing gigantic tracts of trees.
Diaphragmatic lake on the forest shore, deep sulcus cavity of massive sustenance.

Morning scent of sumac, spruce, and sycamore in the open wood, open airway gates.
Morning scent of sumac, spruce, and sycamore in the closed wood, closed passageway gates.

Foliage chest flush with its clusters of leaves, ornamental leaves.
Foliage chest hinged with its folding doors of expansion.

Tree within a tree; forest angles of manubrium and sternum, rib branches, conifer branches.
Tree within a tree; apical and basal forest lobes, woody-stemmed creepers.

Ax to trunk, saw to branch; forest chop blast; tree death.
Ax to trunk, saw to branch; forest cut pruned; tree death.

Tongues of roots tunnel through the ground, tongues of branches tunnel through the air; tree bones.
Tongues of roots tunnel through the ground, tongues of branches tunnel through the air; tree muscles.

Wax fall leaves dropping, dripping from the burning candle tree; colorful forest force of autumn.
Wax fall leaves dropping, dripping from the burning candle tree; colorful forest flame of fall.

Tiny, heaving lungs of the forest beetle, grasshopper, cricket, and worker bee.
Tiny, heaving lungs of the forest insect waltz or minuet.

Grove winds of light; leaf magnet, leaf particle, leaf heat.
Grove winds of light; leaf wave, leaf surge, leaf billow, leaf electricity.

The bright orange sun setting through the trees; forest cooling expiration.
The bright orange sun setting through the trees; cooling winds from the slow spin of the earth.

Bone, wood, ligament, and pulp; architecture of lung leaf.
Bone, wood, ligament, and pulp; cavernous cavity, the sinus of a lung leaf.

Dreamland, forestland; unconscious breath of sleep in the closed country woods.
Dreamland, forestland; dilating, waking woodland wind.

Brothers of the forest; arms of trees, barrels of guns, lungs of liberty.
Brothers of the forest; triggers of twigs, bullets of lead, lungs of freedom.

Land of leaves, multiple lungs on a stem; the leaf replacement and regrowth of manifold leaves.
Land of leaves, multiple lungs on a stem; leaf regions and divisions of multiplex leaves.

Deep, deep forest phonation; a breathy inspiration of the unvoice.
Deep, deep forest phonation; hoarse rustles of shimmers and shakes.

Forest fossa, forest foramina, forest fissure; lair of fox, den of fox, smell of fox.
Forest fossa, forest foramina, forest fissure; lair of air, den of air, smell of air.

The tenderness of timber; scent of sawdust and beauty's grain of wood.
The tenderness of timber; smooth airways of appeal, odors of varnish.

Fibrous tree tissue ring, wreath of winds, hardwood heart.
Fibrous tree tissue ring, skinned leaves of garland, spirit outflow.

Bellies of leaves; compressed leaves, aligned leaves, depressed leaves.
Bellies of air; belly gaps, belly openings, belly holes, belly spaces.

The washings and brushings of dew, islands, and showers of forest beads, pearls, jewels, and stones.
The washings and brushings of dew, Mother Nature's rosary; drops condense on a tree's collar necklace.

Three atrial forest chambers; dome of oak, dome of willow, dome of elm.
Three atrial forest chambers; gust of oak, gust of willow, gust of elm.

Fat forest; the heavy breathing obesity of confusion and disarray.
Fat forest; the pollen breath of a diabetic forest.

Pools of forest winds; the blow, the whisper, the kiss under the lesser wing of pine.
Pools of forest winds; tooth-like projections of a current bower bending branch bite.

As the forest breathes in patterns, inhalation by warm sunlight, inhalation by cool moonlight. As the forest breathes in patterns, exhalation of cold rain, exhalation of hot lightning and thunder.

Cloak of bark, cloak of snowdrifts; slow, naked breathing in and out of breaths of snow. Cloak of bark, cloak of leaves; rapid, clothed breathing in and out of breaths of leaves.

Walking through the woods, dog panting, tree panting, forest panting. Walking through the woods, leg movement, trunk movement, branch movement.

Forest images, the greens and browns smell of the oil of a forest painting. Forest images, the black and white smell of the ink of a forest photograph.

Forest floorboards, the wooden pegs and nails of roots hammered deep within the ground. Forest floorboards, windpipe forest lung branches welded deep from the root of a tree's neck.

The woods are white, white as stone, white as steam, white as a snowflake. The woods are white, white as birch bark, white as dandelion seed, white as spider's silk.

Woodworker as father, Woodworker as Father, the third day, the forest rests. Woodworker as father, Woodworker as Father, cross, thorn, nail, the forest rests.

Boat-shaped leaves with their ribs all floating on currents of forest winds. Boat-shaped leaves with their ribs all holding cups of sunlight, waves of sunlight.

A Lithuanian term "medis" meaning tree; mad is; lost in the woods; wood. A Lithuanian term "medis" meaning tree; airs of medicine.

Spoken Lithuanian "miškas" meaning forest; shade, shadow, ship, sheriff, shoal, shock. Spoken Lithuanian "miškas" meaning forest; shudder, shake, shear, shoulder, shallow, shame.

Forest, chest-like, breast-like nipples of pine cones. Forest, chest-like, breast-like nipples of chestnuts.

Forest mind vapors stream with forest thoughts; green thoughts. Forest mind vapors stream with forest thoughts; virgin thoughts.

Forest legends of staff, spear, shield, sword, and bow and arrow. Forest legends of ancient atmospheres, medieval atmospheres, and atmospheres of the new world.

Andrew G. Zubinas

Intrinsic bowels of the forest, gurgles and bubbles of forest air.
Intrinsic bowels of the forest, gurgles and bubbles of forest light.

Forest pathway breaths, dilation of spring and summer leaves, forest bronchus trail.
Forest pathway breaths, constriction of fall and winter barrenness, forest bronchus trail.

The forest as harbor, masts of the oceans of trees.
The forest as harbor, sails of the oceans of leaves.

Gnarled bark of trees, wrinkles of hands, wrinkles of lungs.
Gnarled bark of trees, curves of weathers, curves of seasons.

Rock-like tree, pebble-like kidney stones and gallstones on the forest bed.
Rock-like tree, pebble-like kidney stones and gallstones on the riverbed.

Tilted trees, Mother Nature's mold.
Tilted trees, Mother Nature's slant.

Straps of forest muscle, tree muscle, disgorging green, the color green.
Straps of forest muscle, tree muscle, straps of stem muscle, leaf muscle.

Plume of forest, plume of lung; feather as leaf as air sac.
Plume of forest, plume of lung; pith of feather, pith of leaf, pith of air sac.

Branches spine-tipped; bottomland forest sits, softwood breathing.
Branches spine-tipped; upland forest runs, hardwood breathing.

Forest life swallows forest life, as involuntary as the midvein and midrib tides.
Forest life swallows forest life, shallow swallow, deep swallow.

Scope of the forest; thin trunk, thin trunk, thin trunk, thick trunk, charred trunk.
Scope of the forest; thin lung, slim lung, skinny lung, thick lung, charred lung.

Views from a ventilating valley; barefoot leaves, barefoot toes.
Views from a ventilating valley; free forest foliage forging sunbeams of steel.

Forest inhalation; conidium, hypha, or spore.
Forest inhalation; aerial, spherule, bud, vesicle, capsule, and filament.

Forest whole, objective forest world; breaths of pain, breaths of pleasure, breaths of reality.

Forest whole, objective forest world; breaths of identity, breaths of excitation, breaths of gratification.

Wood jaw, corners of the forest, green smile articulating words of wood.

Wood jaw, corners of the forest, brown sneer articulating words of wood.

Base, origin, source of a brown tree; the gray cloud exhales roots of lightning.

Base, origin, source of a brown tree; the green forest roots inhale the rain.

Concave, convex woods; the crisp oxygen flow of a forest aqueduct.

Concave, convex woods; bridging drains travel through courses of chasms.

Aged in oak, the moonshine whiskey breathing of a drunken forest.

Aged in oak, the sober forest sobs, drained forest body.

Amber sun, blue granite sky, quartz cloud, emerald leaf, amber trunk; breathing streams of color.

Amber sun, blue granite sky, quartz cloud, emerald leaf, amber trunk; breathing canals of color.

Lightning bolt, trunk shoot, branch shoot, leaf shoot; salty, sudden, severe tempest tree tears.

Lightning bolt, trunk shoot, branch shoot, leaf shoot; sprint, run, or jog of exhaust.

Seed from the shoulders of a tree, infant suckling sapling catches his breath.

Seed from the shoulders of a tree, young lung rhetoric, juvenile lung speech, green lung creed.

The distress of drought, parched plants inundated by dry, hot respiration.

The distress of drought, nerves of wind blow fire, combustible forest.

Long winded tall tales of forest magic, forests of elf and goblin and wizard, mystery winds.

Long winded tall tales of forest magic, forests of troll and fairy and gargoyle, mystery winds.

Read the tea leaves of the forest, aroma signature of herb and spice.

Read the tea leaves of the forest, fire kettle aroma of simmering tea, forest tea.

Frenulum of trunk, tongue-tied tree, the wind makes the leaves rumble and ring and rustle.

Frenulum of trunk, the wind whips, the willow weeps, the water washes.

Deep structures of the forest, green-stained glass of life's architecture.
Deep structures of the forest, a gallery of column growth, pressures in the classical, in the gothic.

Forest sway, the greater horn of wind, the lesser horn of wind.
Forest sway, the red maple leaf cape with the winds of a bullfight, taming twig toreador.

Maimed, disabled forest; factory smokestack escalating to toxicity.
Maimed, disabled forest; chimney airways of the industrial revolution.

"Vainikas," a Lithuanian word of consciousness; circle wreath, anastomoses garland.
"Vainikas," a Lithuanian word of consciousness; saccular, berry aneurysms of leaves.

Forest setting, airway setting; the prominence of a choking tyrant tree.
Forest setting, airway setting; the sparing rigidity of a tyrant tree.

Forest site, lung location; the unopposed forest breathes a breath of pull.
Forest site, lung location; the unopposed forest breathes a breath of push.

Forest black bear and cub; whirlwind of paw, claw, and snout.
Forest black bear and cub; winter overbite, silent manner breathing, sleeping.

Forest trees in full leaf, forest breath holding.
Forest trees in full leaf, fall and winter season sedatives, narcotics, tranquilizers, and relaxants.

Covered in breathy gold leaf; in drawing blankets and sheets; awake, neutral, progressive leaves.
Covered in breathy gold leaf; filtering and cleansing the green tone, green voice, green flush.

Dwarf gnome copse of trees, muffled breath and sound of a forest inlet.
Dwarf gnome copse of trees, mottled, minute, miniscule forest lung lingula of a solitary formation.

Forest winds of the hunt, forest owl and forest mouse, forest wolf and forest hare.
Forest winds of the hunt, forest spider and forest moth, forest robin and firefly, ladybug, and caterpillar.

The forest pharmacy of petals and perfumes and powders and potions and preparations.
The forest pharmacy of the belladonna pupil, the foxglove digit fibrillation and congestive contractility.

The wood's melting pot, the genus and species names in Latin breaths, Latin prayers.
The wood's cauldron, uncountable cotyledon lungs igniting with life.

Resonant, acoustic, voicing kingdom, this side of the forest.
Resonant, acoustic, voicing kingdom, the other side of the forest.

Hunting ground theater, the woodwind and brass echoes of a symphony of moving leaves.
Hunting ground theater, the electric tones of a band of moving leaves.

The living language of the forest; hushing, whispering, muttering paragraphs of life.
The living language of the forest; yelling, shouting, screaming paragraphs of being.

Forest feast; wooden spoon, wooden plate, wooden cup.
Forest feast; smell of festival, smell of banquet, smell of mead.

Giant timberland sponge of forest, not void, not empty, not deserted.
Giant timberland sponge of lung, soft and malleable, filled with oceans of air.

Runaway laughing lungs of mischief; peaseblossom, cobweb, moth, and mustard seed.
Runaway laughing lungs of melancholy; shepherdess, shepherd, country girl, and country man.

Forest to ocean, lung to heart; artery white cloud, artery black cloud, silver vein rain, thunder heartbeat.
Forest to ocean, lung to heart; the hypertensive dry forest cries, flooded with the drops of bronze sun.

Past swish of hoof, neighboring Wood Dale, Woodfield, Woodridge, and Woodstock.
Past swish of hoof, neighboring Lake Forest, Oak Forest, Oak Lawn, Oak Park, and Oak Brook.

Forest star winds; not love nor war, not Venus nor Mars, forest, not human.
Forest star winds; oxlip and cowslip fill the carpenter ant, field ant, fire ant, and pharaoh ant sky.

Forest lettering of winds; grove as grief, grave, grub, greet, growl, group, grape, grail, and growth.
Forest lettering of winds; green as great, grasp, grin, grit, groove, grease, greed, greave, and Greek.

Forest view, breathless insect compound sight view, symmetrical looks of spider eyes, flight of vision.

Forest view, heft of skier, heft of hiker, heft of ranger, the sigh of vision.

Forest moon, forest moan, tucked in the forest bed with a forest bed yawn.

Forest moon, forest moan, shadows and shades and silhouettes of the groaning dusk.

The forest floor chews, belches, and burps with upper lip root and upper teeth roots.

The forest floor chews, belches, and burps with digestive airs of mulch, fresh sod, and mulch.

Forest commune; laws of the elders, the commons, the tribes; free breathing.

Forest commune; fences of the elders, the commons, the tribes; free breathing.

Invited forest, "Kūčios," the Lithuanian term for Christmas Eve, "Kalėdos," meaning Christmas.

Invited forest, a decorated Christmas tree with Lithuanian straw ornaments, white ornaments.

Wooden egg, wood's ovum; pocket of blueberry and blackberry, pouch of strawberry and raspberry.

Wooden egg, wood's ovum; patch of gooseberry and boysenberry, pail of cranberry; empty forest wind.

Early-morning summer stridor, the harsh, rough, course cry of crow.

Early-morning summer stridor, the crow voice box, crow chatterbox, the forest voice box, chatterbox.

Forest decree; fable, story, tale, play crown of Oberon and throne of Titania.

Forest decree; dispatcher, the pursuit, knight on horseback, gales of messages and communication.

In the young child, forest child; absent nose, accessory nose, cleft nose, midface tree knot.

In the young child, forest child; deformity of nose, notching of tip of nose, nose perforation, knot of tree.

Spotted leaf, spotted lung; café au lait or cayenne pepper or purpuric or ruby leaf.

Spotted leaf, spotted lung; black or pigmented or atrophic or regular or irregular leaf.

Mirror of a forest, tree, or leaf in a raindrop.

Mirror of a wind, a breeze, or a gust in a lung drop.

Inflammatory forest bees, the honeycombing sarcoidosis of a sunburnt, sundried, sun-eaten leaf.
Inflammatory forest bees, the honey bee, bumblebee beeswax cough of the woods.

Lungs of lumber; honey breath, wildflower breath, dew breath, sap breath, barley breath.
Lungs of lumber; breath of leaf, breath of stem, breath of bark, breath of root; sweet, succulent scent.

Twisted tangles of trees, Mother Nature's braids spinning, swirling in the web-like wind.
Twisted tangles of trees, thick trunk threads woven by the whittling wind.

Forest staircase of trees, railings from the main trunks, branch steps, rales of wind.
Forest staircase of trees, brown squirrel climbing, crawling up branch steps, the sound of claw.

Woods as cystic, woods as fibrosis; plug of frost, plug of fog, plug of smoke.
Woods as cystic, woods as fibrosis; inborn soil sweat of salt, mineral, and dew.

Forest lumen, lumber lumen; no road, no path, no trail, machete making airway.
Forest lumen, lumber lumen; eddy road, eddy path, eddy trail, maze of winds, ways of winds.

Forest window of willow, wind filled wing of wasp, hive window, lung window.
Forest window of willow, living glass figure of life, absorbing prism of forest light.

Pulmonary plant, flutter of green leaf, flutter of blue jay, flutter of violet flower.
Pulmonary plant, swelling expansion, the turgor of tree.

Tall trees; tower tips touch the churning cloud stomach sky.
Tall trees; the limits of forest height, three stories high, lung length, the lark flies above.

Language, land, larynx, lumber, lung; cords of trees, folds of leaflets, cartilage stump.
Language, land, larynx, lumber, lung; steeple silhouette of a croup cry.

Forest form; wax, wood, stone.
Forest form; humid form, dry form; healthy form, diseased form.

The forest breath bathes a poor healing, widening wooden airway with a dose of bitter tea rootlets.
The forest breath bathes changing patterns of fat-laden, omega-shaped, club-shaped sloughing leaves.

The ventilating drive of the forest hollows, the yield of air.
The ventilating drive of the forest hollows, unroofed and headless, without skullcap.

Forest spike; thorn of rose, stinger of bee; rapid respiratory rate.
Forest spike; nail of raccoon, tooth of opossum; rapid respiratory rate.

Forked branches, forked limbs of lung.
Forked branches, forked guts of the forest.

Forest arch major; the grove grunts as the treetop impost sinks the treasure tree trunk into the soil.
Forest arch minor; streaks of veins, its leaf fashioned as a reverse ogee arch in the temple of a tree.

Encircling forest; tick and tock breath of a pair of wound cuckoo clock branches, clock hands.
Encircling forest; engulfing, asphyxiating the stagnant fossil ruins of a forgotten city; feeding forest.

The wood's moon marrow, the howl of wind, the howl of wolf strike to the core of one's bones.
The wood's moon marrow, campfire answers moonlight and starlight before the red marrow daybreak.

The frozen forest thaws; outer heat, warming lung, inner cold, cold lung.
The frozen forest thaws; spring drops, descending breath drops, arising dripping development.

Imbibing forest, the cream and sugar of a freshly brewed cup of forest coffee.
Imbibing forest, the clouds and winds of a freshly brewed cup of forest coffee.

Forest air cell, cage cell; spring winds damage winter, summer winds damage spring.
Forest air cell, cage cell; fall winds damage summer, winter winds damage fall.

Witch wood; reigning spell, clouded chant, tree trance, wand of wind.
Witch wood; old, sinister, malicious, bad, evil, wicked, devil working lungs.

Wind in a tree's hair; mustache of moss, beard of bark.
Wind in a tree's hair; goosebump limb hair and nest chest hair.

The wood's circles; splash and splatter and shallows of rain.
The wood's circles; collective, winds conveyed; raincloud sphincter.

Drenched forest sun pneumonia raining, drowned deep, wet and soggy.
Drenched forest sun pneumonia raining, spreading with millions and millions of raindrops.

Paired, the forest monarch butterfly spreads its black and orange lungs.
Paired, the forest dragonfly spreads its clear and fragile lungs.

The forest coat of arms, lung shield with its chemical combat and war-torn nodules.
The forest coat of arms, voice cushion lung shield.

Vast forest and the mew cri du chat, newborn mew.
Vast forest and the birdsong of a sparrow, lung song.

The forest faints, dry and fractured leaves on the ground.
The forest faints, fall knocks the pale wind out of the trees that are drained of green.

The floating forest cotyledon cloud, roots of light, soil of dark, moist raincloud, silver dew-lined soil.
The floating forest cotyledon cloud, the seed fan gracefully glides to the ground.

Taxing throat tree of pipe and flute and trumpet.
Taxing throat tree of soprano chirp and tenor rustle and baritone growl.

Forest senses, a second wind.
Forest senses, a second of time.

Stemming from the forest, multiple abscesses, gangrenous and necrotic, entrapped and encysted debris.
Stemming from the forest, teething, fibrinous dim light, dim wind.

Ground garment, air trapping apron ditch of leaves.
Ground garment, overlying forest, overcompensating, overgrown, and overdeveloped.

Forest stream, gilled mushrooms and barnacles of stone.
Forest stream, the airflow thought and the water flow thought of the forest mind.

Forest pump, a full Windsor necktie knot of pulmonary arteries and veins.
Forest pump, congestive and restrictive, the woods germinate unchecked and unrestrained.

The cool, cool forest numbness, the ascending force of air, the force of white.
The cool, cool forest numbness, the descending leaves falling from the tingling trees.

Borderless forest, Lithuanian "kiškis" for rabbit, "vilkas" for wolf, "meška" for bear, and "lapė" for fox.
Borderless forest, Lithuanian "briedis" for moose, "šernas" for boar, and "voverė" for squirrel.

Exercise of wind, trapezius treetop forest swagger.
Exercise of wind, triceps tree extension of green, heavy leaf green.

The wood's barred sides, crib form, baby form, infant form, forest form, wind form.
The wood's barred sides, cradle sapling umbilicus knot.

Parenchyma of the forest, the trees; results in cough, fever, and dyspnea.
Parenchyma of the forest, the trees; results in the green stone-like wall, wood wall.

Without rustles, the difficulty speaking Indian summer calm breathing of the forest.
Without rustles, the difficulty speaking indigenous names of rivers and lakes.

Pinching the nares, forest air hunger takes root.
Pinching the nares, forest blowhard reflex, root reflex.

Traveling through the wood; routes of roots underfoot.
Traveling through the wood; footprint, paw print, horseshoe print, bird and worm prints, all lung prints.

The whale skin of a tree; the skin of lung, the eye of lung, the tail of lung, the calf of lung.
The whale skin of a tree; the forest whale, the forest sea, the forest green-brown ripples and wrinkles.

Inside the forest, via the crust and crest of air, forest invagination.
Inside the forest, via the long and narrow parts, forest invagination.

Anchored branches, inflexible and rigid short head in the water wind.
Anchored branches, flexible and pliable long head in the water wind.

Dried leaves crunched and crumpled into a bronze powder.
Dried leaves etching the shapes of the forest breath.

Forest cleft, crag, and crevice in a cathedral of cedars, obelisk-like in a grove of minarets.
Forest cleft, passing deep, lung wane of a sickle-like briar, a crescent-like briar.

Forest face; brow furrows, leafy frown lines, crow's feet, spindle pine needle eyelashes.
Forest face; the lung cheeks' uncontrollable cough.

Cleansing forest trough; inhalation of the good, the short arm of the forest wind.
Cleansing forest peak; exhalation of the bad, the long arm of the forest wind.

Laminar lung flow, line of wind marching in the forest.
Laminar lung flow, line of tree standing in the forest.

Pine needle sensation of pinpricks, the sensation of wind, the sensation of drizzle.
Pine needle fine structure, brush structure, comb structure, wind structure, rain structure.

The segmental, lobar, and whole weight loss of autumn.
The segmental gemstone tint and dye injections of fall with its colored collapsing lung.

Inflated and dilated, juices and nectars of teardrops springing forth from the forest chest pain.
Inflated and dilated, forest oriole and mockingbird swoop and swish and swoosh and swirl.

The fourth and sixth forest arches; relations of winds enter below the keel-shaped roof.
The fourth and sixth forest arches; a residing series of winds.

Forest eye, right; the cloudy eye of sky.
Forest eye, left; the forest green lungs in an eagle's eye.

Forest heart formation, malformation; winds migrate, buds ascend to their final position.
Forest heart formation, malformation; tearing winds rupture and break the soil plate.

"Žalias" for green, "giria" for forest; the Grand Duke of the Duchy of Lithuania, "mūšis" for battle.
"Žalias" for green, "giria" for forest; the Grand Master of the Order of the Teutonic Knights, "mūšis."

Uvula of the fleshy forest, dangling wolf spider descending into the neck of the woods.
Uvula of the fleshy forest, cocooned bug ensnared in a deadly forest snore, a forest web of sleep.

The beekeeper's veil with the bee breath and buzz, the odor of insect incense.

The beekeeper's veil with the queen bee and her flower, her colony, her forest.

Polymorphic, pleomorphic forest; the gland-like intestinal type wood dust tumor of the nasal sinuses.

Polymorphic, pleomorphic forest; tobacco plaques and keratin pearls; verrucous or basaloid, spindle.

Eden forest, four forest rivers; Pishon, Gihon, Tigris, Euphrates.

Eden forest, five forest lobes; three lung lobes on the right, two lung lobes on the left.

Dressed in ribbons of leaves, in dancing attire, the treetops dance in the wind with the zinc stars.

Dressed in ribbons of leaves, dressed in heartbeats, the lung maypoles dance slow and sway-like.

Encapsulated forest, the slow blinking eyelid of the breathtaking brassy sunrise voice.

Encapsulated forest, forest framework contoured with a lung winter involution.

Barking cough, a small pond's auscultation of the forest breath sounds.

Barking cough, the rumble of a herniated river, the rumble of thunder, of wind.

Forest lesion, lung lesion-stained summer green; leaf ribbons, cords, trabeculae, rosettes, nests.

Forest lesion, lung lesion-stained cold; central or peripheral, small or non-small, coin or cannonball.

Forest irritation, the remnant stellate scar of a broken lung forest branch.

Forest irritation, the remnant central scar of a broken lung forest branch.

Misfolded leaves warmed by a ductal system consisting of corpuscles of white light.

Misfolded leaves stratified with thickening signet-ring-like goblets of green, guts of green.

Markings of the wood; animal sniff of wood, animal sniff of territory; mental mark.

Markings of the wood; animal sniff of predator, animal sniff of prey; lung mark.

Forest pounding lung; lightning spark of the forest blacksmith hammer and anvil.

Forest pounding lung; sparked constricting pupil, sparked dampening ossicular chain of the middle ear.

Forest storm, forest spasm; raindrop bulbs deeply bury the forest trauma.

Forest storm, forest spasm; windstorm, rainstorm, thunderstorm, hailstorm, lung storm.

Forest, ajar; open forest treatment, exposed to the environment, visible.
Forest, ajar; the air above the forest lake or forest field; the forest gape.

Uttering forest; naturally unstressed bird lung song, stressed cricket lung stanza.
Uttering forest; forest meter in four seasons, four lung meters.

The orifice of a forest; forest leaf green eyes; forest trunk brown nares; encircling color muscle.
The orifice of a forest; forest leaf red mouth; forest trunk white ears; encircling air muscle.

Emanating embroidered emotion, Russian doll-like spot within wing, insect within leaf, camouflage dew.
Emanating embroidered emotion, tapestry teardrop stolen and sewn from a dew point breath.

Tree of virtues; the leaves point upward toward heaven; red cardinal eating lung meal berry.
Tree of vices; the leaves point downward toward hell; red cardinal eating lung meal worm.

Bronchus and bronchiole railways, a hooting steam engine network of xylem and phloem rays.
Bronchus and bronchiole railways, a rail station voice box pit stop of corded gates and switches.

Spider venom, snake venom, forest venom; pacified lungs, sleeping lungs, paralyzed lungs, quiet lungs.
Spider venom, snake venom, forest venom; the deadly dew drop numbing forest fangs.

Forest stone, active lung stone, post-infectional lung stone, tuberculous lung stone.
Forest stone, rough or smooth, set inside the upside-down calcified crown of topsoil.

Hue of lilac, forest sashes, expanding lung span of a noble and feathered white egret.
Hue of lilac, forest sashes, sword of air, strand of air, pattern of air, knot of air.

Forest fire sunrise breath; copper bark, bronze bark, iron bark, steel bark.
Forest fire sunset breath; forest furnace, forest fever, forest mill, forest industry.

Layered green, an eye's steps of deep digestion.
Layered green, layered lung of pinned, clinging, hanging, and dangling leaves.

Forest fist of wind, a boxing treetop forest sport.
Forest fist of wind, a knocking cleanliness forest bath.

Forest spools of wind, breathing patterns, threads of breeze, stitched gusts.
Forest spools of wind, lung working spinning wheel breaths sewn in leaf flax and leaf yarn.

Crossed and uncrossed wind mapping tree line impressions.
Crossed and uncrossed prolonged speaking wind, a sound stream sliver buried into the forest skin.

Following infusion, perfusion, or transfusion; the jasmine or emerald forest air.
Following infusion, perfusion, or transfusion; the leaf drink bubbles, clear bubbles.

Mixed or pure, forest growth; pinnate lung as flat, as sessile, as pedunculated
Mixed or pure, forest growth; broadleaf lung as works, as factory, as mill, as manufactury.

Bent tree, wind-induced knee bend-like, river bend-like, toad trail bend-like.
Bent tree, wind-induced sycamore spring.

Ungoverned grove lobe, a casting innervation by seed and pod and fruit.
Ungoverned grove lobe, a small labyrinthine air abyss of oval.

Inside a hand lens, a forest fixation; serially sliced chunks of forest, a thick slice.
Inside a hand lens, a forest fixation; sagittally sliced chunks of green, forest green vision adhesions.

Adventitious forest sounds; fowl rhonchi, warbler wheeze, robin rale and rub, tweeting trees.
Adventitious forest roots; veering root, laborious root, loud root, explosive root, root burst.

A timid creature, a spider retreats.
A timid creature, one pair of book lungs.

Envenomation, real or imagined; summer light forest venom, forest burn.
Envenomation, real or imagined; autumn frost forest venom, forest surfactant.

A red leaf, the pitch break and voice arrest of summer.
A red leaf, the shaky, quivering quality of fall's sighs.

Bark pore, bark lenticel, the drainage point of a wind stream, lung point.
Bark pore, bark lenticel, lens spot, breath spot without shutter, the wooded spot easel.

Pneumatic pine, maple meatus, redwood recess, sycamore sinus.
Pneumatic pine, junction of air and mind.

Forest, immobile; the trunk remains steadfast as the treetops rock and wobble.
Forest, immobile; firm honeysuckle peace pipe lung treaty, the motion of smoke.

Stabbing wind, the blister green of a spring onset.
Stabbing wind, the white boils and ulcers of a winter onset.

Notch of the woods, swells of rain green respiration.
Notch of the woods, longer than wide, the middle of a word, forest word.

Loops of the woods, loop of green nourishment in between the circles of winds.
Loops of the woods, the round ring of winter's reduced sensation.

The fresh air of the sumac's salts and soaps.
The fresh air impacted.

Semilunar wood; leaf oblong, elliptical, ovate, and obtuse.
Semilunar wood; wind doubly toothed, smooth, and tapering.

Calculi in the soil amongst the ironwood and the hawthorn and the beech.
Calculi in the soil amongst the mulberry and the ash and the cottonwood.

Autumn's anemia, autumn's ache, autumn's agony, autumn's anguish, autumn's ailment.
Autumn's anemia, fall's fatigue, November's numbness, dampening respiration.

Disc of sun, disc of moon, disc of lake in the forest bloodstream of wind.
Disc of gold, of silver, of blue in the biconcave Janus faces of the wooden day arch and stone night arch.

Breathing in the green rash of spring lung and the non-green rash of autumn lung.
Breathing out the disappearance.

Lithuanian "spalva" for color, "spalis" for the month of color.
Lithuanian "lapas" for leaf, "kristi" for fall or drop, "lapkritis" for the month of leaf drop.

Beehive lung chandelier; honey-like mud or fire, honey-like edema, honey-like ointment or lavage.
Beehive lung chandelier; honey-like herniation or probe, honey-like bud or airflow.

The tree posture with its never resting chest rising and falling.
The tree posture with its polyphonic vocal intensity spoken through slow, slow season strained colors.

Forest function; tree number, tree size, tree connections.
Forest function; a cause, a consequence, a compensation, a confound.

A convergence into forest; neural bird flock, neural wolf pack, neural bee swarm, neural ant hill.
A convergence into forest; tree dirt divergence; respiratory reciprocity scene.

Rook of knock and knob, node and nook.
Rook of oak, the silent solitary sentinel strength.

Forest bifurcation, snake-like.
Forest bifurcation, snake tongue-like, the wind tells lies.

A season's song, the forest vocal folds calloused like the hands of a farmer.
A season's song, the forest vocal harshness and frailties of the wilderness.

Tree hill, hump, hummock, hillock, and hilus.
Tree hill, the thick fortress walls, stronghold battlements, and citadel towers of a castle hill.

Forest translation, forest sea, Lithuanian "jūra" for sea, sailor's sea lung.
Forest translation, forest farm, Lithuanian "ūkis" for farm, farmer's farm lung.

The feel, the sound of the midrange forest mouthparts' winter timbre.
The feel, the sound of the fuzzy leaf uproar and clamor in reply to jostling, juggling, jittering currents.

The drooping eyelid lung branch of a fir tree, fir tree needle net.
The drooping eyelid lung branch of a fir tree, fir tree rabbit foot slipper of stubble.

Mechanical tree, mechanical life; fiber filament flesh flow.
Mechanical tree, mechanical life; the blood gush of dawn.

Elevating elm; eyes raised, neck raised, lung raised, a healing fountain.
Elevating elm; wrinkles across the forehead, wrinkles across the land.

Clear day, clear wood, clear lung; fall golden onion dome leaves set against a deep blue sky.
Clear day, clear wood, clear lung; fall air understandable, fall air comprehensible and transparent.

Hunts at night; red eyes, black bill, heron black back, mantle, and crown.
Hunts at night; the trembling, shaking chest of a yellow-legged heron.

"Malda," Lithuanian for prayer, a psalm plant in the house of the Lord.
"Malda," Lithuanian for prayer, "Dievas" for the Deity, the Supreme Being, "dievulis" for god.

An iron wolf; a nobleman's dream, a forest dream.
An iron wolf; breath of sleep, breath of dream, breath of iron, breath of wolf, the breath of Vilnius.

Forest gait, walk of duck, crawl of centipede, gallop of unicorn, hop of grasshopper.
Forest gait, lungs filled to the brim.

Millipede-like arms of trees, a wind footing with breezes of string, pulley, and rope.
Millipede-like arms of trees, a lung span balanced and bilateral.

Gem carving forest studs; goldsmith sun, silversmith moon, lung medallions.
Gem carving forest stripes; braided goldwork sunbeams, mosaic inlay silverwork moonbeams.

The scratchy sound of leaves during the mood swings of the seasons.
The scratchy sound of leaves played on a wind instrument with double reeds.

Altered forest voice; spring song bud blends.
Altered forest voice; summer sounds become poor, fall breathy breaks invert to a silent white wood.

Pollen and seed and nut of the wood thrown by a sling of wind.
Pollen and seed and nut of the wood torn by a swallow of wind.

The rainforest sleeps, an African eye closes, the tse-tse eye remains open.
The rainforest sleeps, tse-tse twilight lullaby, burrowed nightmares.

Andrew G. Zubinas

The horizon breaks open, the forest breath formation breaks open, the pinnacle lung breaks open.

The horizon breaks open, an autumn blood-like treetop tapestry, the bearing bronchiole bone branches.

Jaw in miniature, earthworm taste of soil, insect taste of leaf, hummingbird and nightingale taste of air.

Jaw in miniature, lung in miniature, Mother Nature's doll house in miniature.

Forest without manifest; before the leaves turn, before they exhale pigments.

Forest without manifest; before the overload of buds, before the chrome wood develops green hunger.

An army of cloud, wave and wave, lung and lung of silver, gray, black, and white.

An army of cloud, raindrops fill an empty nest as the clouds part.

Sheath of lung bark, wet investing layer pleurisy of poplar or pine.

Sheath of lung bark, the encasing wine cork cushion of a cloth-covered conduit.

Forest country, wooden amoeba emblem of bleb or blurb, blotch or blob, amoeba of blot.

Forest country, the linguistics and languages of lung, foreign forest lung.

Deep tendon, deep timber; deep breath, timber breath.

Deep tendon, deep timber; deep green, timber brown.

Stone-like wind, buckeye deposits in the tubules of the woods.

Stone-like wind, acorn deposits in the tubules of the woods.

Nests of light, Mother Nature's braids of lightning.

Nests of light, heated eggshell lung sacs.

Lung lakes, gripped betwixt the northern woods, an isthmus of the Great Lakes.

Lung lakes, the five lobes of Huron, Ontario, Michigan, Erie, and Superior.

Eight slender spiny rib-like legs, ensnared infiltrates of gnat, moth, mosquito, fly, and butterfly.

Eight slender spiny rib-like legs, ensnared infiltrates of forest critters and creatures.

Open lung, a naked leaf brewing juices and light within a linen leaf cloth inside a leaf chalice.

Open lung, a naked leaf breathing heat and air within a green lacework inside a leaf altar.

Saddled with leaves, saddled with occlusion, saddled with clot.
Saddled with needles, the pyemic, pyogenic pines litter the ground.

Tree by type, by effect, by presence.
Tree by birth, by mother, by lung.

Diffused through lighted leaves, wading winds, soaked soils, and head halos of clouds.
Diffused particulates snowballed into a magnetic-like mass, a grit globe, a rib indented onion-like orb.

Siberian lily of the field; petals of moonstone, golden stem, golden stamens, tipped with diamonds.
Siberian lily of the field; cold lungs of mesmerism, hypnotism, braidism, somnambulism, magnetism.

Rainy oration phonetic segments; brown trees thick with shortened daylight; fall's facial grimace.
Rainy oration phonetic segments; water immersed, hemorrhagic leaves adhere to the gagging ground.

A tendency toward excess, the green mania of summer, the white depression of winter.
A tendency toward excess, leaf building blocks of overindulgence, immoderation, and extravagance.

Coiled trees; a fine-tune jitter and shimmer, expansion and retrusion.
Coiled trees; a skeletonizing mainstem elastic, the coiled caliber of the airways.

Haphazard, yet intercalated, the landmark framework bronchovascular bundles of birch and beech.
Haphazard, yet intercalated, a straight path, a straight course of cedar C-rings.

Ford the winds, the raked rivers of fallen leaves.
Ford the winds, the reeking rivers of a skunk's signature.

Chronic and obstructive, color of forest emerald, color of forest amber, liquid-like lung stone scene.
Chronic and obstructive, the healing arts of the jeweler, stonecutter, sculptor, and smith.

Asthma of ants and bees; sphincter of anthill, sphincter of beehive, a bronchoconstriction.
Asthma of ants and bees; heated hill or hive.

Rugose and ruffled forest floor, the never-resting early childhood lungs of a moss-like sapling playpen.

Rugose and ruffled forest floor, breeze-backed, corrugated cobblestone curbs and coral-covered curves.

The chimes of leaves, the whispering woodland mounts and climbs into a gong cough.

The chimes of leaves, crescendo of spring, sustained summer, decrescendo fall; coda, cold and colorless.

Cochlear cough, softspoken sway of treetops in the forest windows.

Cochlear cough, whitecap waves of wind dislodge an acorn, a cochlear acorn seashell.

Forest path, the zig and zag of leaf, airways of acorns, pinecone projection.

Forest path, a coyote runs parallel to a forest fence, the fox trots elsewhere.

Leaves in clonus, a gentle wind.

Leaves in clonus, the limb load and lift.

Balanced breathing, a moon heart's cusp cycles, balanced time, a lung forest's sine of the sun.

Balanced breathing, in chipmunk color, an acrobatic autumn.

Forest entrapment, clawed canopy, the white cloud fingernail tips of brown forest fingers.

Forest entrapment, the tree temptation of forest freshness, forest froth.

Mingling maples, the snow gowns and night suits of a forest ballroom dance.

Mingling maples, brotherhood breath, a tavern team of trees.

Buried beneath a color continuum, the tongues of trees in autumn's acoustic amplified aperture.

Buried beneath a color continuum, verbal and visual, forest footplate flair, cistern canopy cul-de-sac.

Fall in New England, the pure gold bullion boughs and lobster-like looking leaves.

Fall in New England, log volumes of trunks and treasures, independent and trading tides.

A rotation of growth, the rim and hub of leaves, branch spokes and axels of sun and moon.

A rotation of growth, a life wheel mired and marooned.

The late effect of fall, a barren and bleak brow.

The late effect of fall, out of breath at the staircase summit.

In the presence of pine, the tingling smell of a pine's needlework.
In the presence of pine, the layers of strength, heavy royal green.

The babbling leaves, the fat-like spaces betwixt the leaves, highly vacuolated.
The babbling leaves, wind thought turns to forest speech.

Communicating, web-like, orbit spun, a bone white cocooned moon, silver suspended rib moonlight.
Communicating, web-like, the vein leaf ultrastructure; the noncommunicating autumn aquarium leaves.

The granulation of the soil, the breathing weather vestiges of the vascular forest ground.
The granulation of the soil, the clods, clumps, and clots of the frozen December forest ground.

Protruding forest eyes, like fly, like chimera.
Protruding forest eyes, like a quiet and forced sunrise inspiration.

The lethargy of the woods, circulating stillness, circulating silence.
The lethargy of the woods, a sunset heart drop.

Palpitations of the pine, the bouncing branch of the resting red-breasted robin.
Palpitations of the pine, excessive sheets of snow fall to the ground off needle branch shields.

A basket formed from forest wicker, flower filled or fruit filled.
A basket formed from forest wicker, a cradle shape of woven wicker wind.

The breathing bursts of the awe of autumn, the advent of autumn.
The breathing bursts of bolts of buds basking in the beams.

Narrow fascicles, narrow icicles; doublets of forested Smolensk and Pskov, forested Riga and Tallinn.
Narrow fascicles, narrow icicles; rod-like Konigsberg and Cracow, disk-like Minsk and Kiev.

Without white birch or evergreen, the cartilage completely disappears in temperate forest passes.
Without white birch or evergreen, the side arms of mahogany brown.

Aged lungs, the staccato of seasons performed through the treble and bass of sunlight.
Aged lungs, an accordion slowness, almost labored bagpipes.

Andrew G. Zubinas

The wind as a scavenger; a warm-blooded wind nibbles on the forest grounds.
The wind as a scavenger; tool of flint, of bone, of hide; tool of arrowhead, of hook, of needle.

Implanted axe, the tree's overt blood-clots of wood chip.
Implanted axe, the tree's spinal cord senses become dull, the tree's breath blunt.

Autumn airways, warmed by the sun, moistened by the moon, the dead space of dawn and dusk.
Autumn airways, a well suited interface of colors, controlled colors inhaled into the upper airways.

The forgotten forest wind follows hawk, follows thrush, follows pigeon, follows sparrow, follows crow.
The forgotten forest wind follows sunrise, rain, and rainbow, follows orchid, ladies'-tresses, and daisy.

Raise the ribs, a respiratory zone of coltsfoot and geranium and bloodroot and violet.
Raise the ribs, a respiratory zone of mints and turtleheads and buttercups and Jack-in-the-Pulpits.

Resorption of the woods, an exit under the white columns of dawn's gate.
Resorption of the woods, Mother Nature's forest face no longer dark or black.

Breathe in, last out, the debits and credits of leaves and colors.
Breathe in, last out, the exchange of coins of air and bills of light.

Forest, northbound; totem pole treetop tails, salmon scales of bark, the fins of a fir tree.
Forest, northbound; tremors of leaves among the raven clan, raven wood, raven respiration.

Residing deep, passing through, forest icy smoke breath of caribou and elk and moose.
Residing deep, passing through, forest trail of salmon, of eagle, of grizzly bear.

A forest flood of dusk's anesthesia, trees in twilight, the trees tarred in black night.
A forest flood of dusk's anesthesia, the breathing dwindles during the summer slumber.

An oak, an upright lung, a tufted column unlike the lichen-covered flat and squamous tundra plateau.
An oak, an upright lung, an upright apple core chair of the wood's noon hour.

The discomfort, pressure, and tightness of a canopy, cramped and crowded.

The discomfort, pressure, and tightness of the Rocky Mountain nipple eyes' breath-holding spell.

A single breath, in leaf, in day, in moon, in season.

A single breath, in forest, in milk of cloud, in sea.

Bulge of buds, after a clean shaven winter, a stubby spring forest face.

Bulge of buds, loose within wind, tight within plant.

The forest, charmer, enchantress; the autumn allure of her high-necked dress.

The forest, charmer, enchantress; her complexion painted in a fall folio of fragrances and fascinations.

The slurred speech spoken and sung by the birch leaves of Žemaitija.

The slurred speech beaten into the woods through the corridors of winds and wars.

Leaves foamy and fibrinous, the blurred heat of an August exudate of malaise.

Leaves foamy and fibrinous, an inhaled focus mummified in fiber bandage banners of green.

A discharge of dew with its rain scent percolating from the forest floor.

A discharge of dew with the overnight moonlight markings minted in petechial perspiration.

A gathered breathing, willow tree crown branches of a Venetian mask.

A gathered breathing, elm tree branches of St. Anne's spires.

Overarched, the torch of the sun is extinguished by the pendulum of the moon.

Overarched, the forest candle is extinguished into fog.

Nodules of acorns fall to the ground after a goiter gust.

Nodules of acorns seed the lymphatics of the lung landscape.

The storm cloud brings quarrel, drooping shoulder movements with the raised voice of the woods.

The storm cloud brings quarrel, the difficult breathing trajectory of a cool autumn argument.

The nest, covered by kingfisher wing, the lung, covered by scapula wing.

The nest, covered by kingfisher wing, the forest, covered by cloud wing.

Soil sagging silver stone, chest cavity countryside contours sagging green, full and filled.
Soil sagging silver stone, wood's surrounding setting sagging sun.

Scant hemoptysis of a red oak, red cedar, red maple, red pine, red mulberry, red bud, and red clover.
Scant hemoptysis of a red fox, red-tailed hawk, red spider, red deer, red salmon, and red squirrel.

The stenosis keyhole of day, forest wintertime myopia.
The stenosis keyhole of night, forest summertime mind.

Failing to thrive, a distorted tree of hickory, longstanding, rickets-like with chest wall sequela.
Failing to thrive, unable to fly after hatching from a demineralized egg.

Pits of bark, notches of nose and neck.
Pits of leaves, alveolar pits of cherries, alveolar pits of plums, alveolar pits of peaches.

Bud-like and bell-like, a handful of sprouting cranial vaults multiplying on a stem.
Bud-like and bell-like, petals like facial muscles, roots like internal lungs, sprigs like icicle eyes.

Lungs intact, the inadequate light of autumn's anorexia.
Lungs intact, marked by pain and tenderness, the fall leaves shrink, starve, and shrivel.

Ends and sides of trees, shaggy or stout or slender.
Ends and sides of trees, the long-tapering midforest woods breathe easy.

The yawn-sigh footsteps on the friable soil, gummatous ground.
The yawn-sigh treeline, swollen and distended as the day shifts to night.

Tendon petals fastened as a snug and cozy neckband.
Tendon petals bound and affixed in between a snowflake skeleton of ribs.

Forest airways paved in crystal, stone, diamond, and quartz.
Forest airways paved in wood, living wood.

The hedgehog hobbles sluggishly, soil secured like honey lava.
The hedgehog hobbles lead-footed, a plodding pair of lungs.

The wind-touched whiskers of a field mouse, of a mountain lion.
The wind-touched needles of a porcupine.

Scepter of rain paired with forest orb.
Scepter of rain expired.

Tear of cloud, stone of cloud, spear of cloud, sphere of cloud, sapphire of cloud.
Tear of cloud, lung tears escalating into a thundercloud cough.

Purpura clouds, dusk sky scars, violaceous sunset scabs, the day's healing bruises or blemishes.
Purpura fields, lavender lungs, lacquered and lake-like.

Bookshelf branches of trees, needle scrolls, leaf scripts, an exhaled expansion.
Bookshelf branches of trees, summer shelved, color inked, rhymes in rustle.

The wind as tensor, a stiff, solidifying chill of the woods.
The wind as tensor, a lodging, retracting tone of timber.

Forest in recurrence, in obstruction, impassible and irreducible, in gangrene.
Forest in recurrence, in sliding moons, in leaf hiatus, in birth.

The umbilical cord moon of an unborn day, an unborn season.
The umbilical cord moon severed with the phoenix sun as the forest breathes day.

The careworn birch bark, garment of Christ, rugged, rough, gnarled, and covered with pockmarks.
The careworn birch bark, written Latin "spiritus" in inspiration, in expiration, in perspiration.

Transcendental forest, Thoreau-like, Emerson-like, Whitman-like.
Transcendental forest, the nineteenth-century American breath of the incorporation of the Windy City.

Intrinsic in rain, intrinsic in green, intrinsic in inspiration.
Intrinsic in rain, "lietus" meaning rain, "Lietuva" meaning Lithuania.

Leaf, sun side or soil side, the porous green membrane of spring and summer.
Leaf, sun side or soil side, above or below.

Regress into a forest primordial sleep.
Regress into a mask of fall color, into a mask of winter snow, into a mask of regressive respiration.

An ectopic and extrinsic eagle dives into the forest green.

An ectopic and extrinsic Eden, the seed of apple inspires generation upon generation upon generation.

Brought to consciousness over crowd, over swarm, over herd, over flock, over forest.

Brought to consciousness through shade and stain, through paint and pigment, through invisible aura.

Two tribunes of sun and moon, the eloquence of the forest assembly.

Two tribunes of sun and moon, the breathing debates of sunlight rhetoric and moonlight oration.

A recollection of the forgotten, the forest lung airways and their passages of time.

A recollection of the forgotten, a south tipped bird formation during the cold months.

Scattered forest floor temples, acorn cap turrets, colorful churchyard carts and carriages of leaves.

Scattered forest floor temples, God's voice box leaves, curled churches, spire-tipped and dome shaped.

The living needle of a worm, the living needlepoint of a mite, forest injected.

The living needle of a pine, the living needlepoint of the top of a tree.

Sunrise saber, sunset scabbard, the breath holding inlet to outlet.

Sunrise saber, sunset scabbard, the forest's grasping achievement.

Frozen wasp nest, with caveolae, with fenestrae, frost fringed, frost frozen.

Frozen wasp plopped on the ground, yellow jackets let fall, let go, like fall leaves.

Body margins of a daffodil, the wooing willpower and wishpower.

Body margins of leaf intake, of forest lake limbus, of an evening's edge.

Lung of loam, a healing erosion.

Lung of loam, tunnel and home of gopher, mole, and groundhog.

Autumn bleeds profusely, sharpened light exhales cut ends, severed ends, cut vessels, severed vessels.

Autumn bleeds profusely, leaves float in the puddles, their stems no longer anchored.

The waterfall effect of the falling leaves, of the falling rain, of the falling fruit, of the falling tree.
The waterfall effect of forest blues and forest reds, cascade cloud white to cloud gray to cloud black.

Free wind, slave wind; lung thrashed, heart struck.
Free wind, slave wind; forest intestines tied and bound.

The emissary moonlight rivulets, white wine pressed for thirty days from the grape of the moon.
The emissary moonlight rivulets, cratered moon sac, half moon deflated, half moon inflated.

The greed of lung and forest; the twin circulations of thirst and hunger.
The greed of lung and forest; the limits and boundaries of cycles, forest lung cycles.

Cancer as forest fruit; cancer as a rotten, spoiled, putrid, necrotic mush.
Cancer as forest fruit; lung fruit deadly seed.

Leaves chatter and chuckle as the female forest widow winds congregate.
Leaves chatter and chuckle as autumn trees unclothe in wait for the virgin snow.

Unilateral disdain thaws to happiness; woods thaw to sapling, pup, chick, and cub.
Unilateral disdain thaws to happiness; wet with life, the spring air is washed new, clean with youth.

With the lower lip everting and with a raising muscle of wind, the poplar pouts.
With the lower lip everting and the forest breath stopping, pouting clouds bring gray and gloom.

Oars of winds move waves of trees.
Oars of lungs in pairs turn and guide the seasons.

Forest sulcus of sadness, no leaf or work after harvest.
Forest sulcus of sadness, non-breathing barren trees with tears turning from dew to frost to snow.

The morphine and barbiturate breathing of winter blue, a short day paralysis without leaf or seed.
The morphine moon, dull and cold, forest nighttime in hypoventilation.

Depleted, the season of shunt, winter's blood flow abolished.
Depleted, the season of shunt, pumped with cold, snow, and ice.

Andrew G. Zubinas

Quill of straw, quill of grass, quill of leaf; alphabet in yellows, in greens, in reds.
Quill of straw, quill of grass, quill of leaf; ballads breath-by-breath, brush-by-brush.

The bumps and barbs of bronchioles; harmonies of hush and howl.
The bumps and barbs of bronchioles; via the boulevard, via the avenue thoroughfare.

Limewood and rosewood canvas, spring snow mottled and marbled.
Limewood and rosewood canvas, spring snow pierced and punctured and perforated.

Intensely stained and unbleached, a sunlit scene.
Intensely stained and uninhibited, a breath of fall.

Chaste tree in the royal forest under forest law.
Chaste tree in absolute abstinence, a crown's cavitation.

Bucket handle of rib, forest water mineral soft, mineral fresh, mineral sweet.
Bucket handle of rib, forest territorial water air stream under a bridge of stone.

Lung-lining, cloud in cage, mirror deep.
Lung-lining, the autumn artery anastomoses of falling leaves exploring the ground.

Suspended in the air, a crow as a black nugget, a gravel-filled skyline.
Suspended in the air, a knotwork of trees against the turquoise.

A season's stealth, the weights and measurements of fall color cold October moon moneybags.
A season's stealth, ledger of light and lung removed.

Off the midline, black cherry tree mammary arteries, mammary bodies.
Off the midline, buckthorn tree vena cava.

The reverse flow of a January warm front, a July cold front.
The reverse flow of tears of air, an upstream flower flow scent constricted with petal dam.

The blind wind reads the braille of bark and beak and bronchiole.
The blind wind of winter without leaf eye exhales darkness, snow and darkness.

The underlying skeleton of moving moon rib arc clutching the cage of night.
The underlying skeleton marrow of unborn raindrops replenishing pale anemic clouds with iron gray.

The twirling dance of winds, the pronator drift of an oak's hand.
The twirling dance of winds, chest whirling, chest skipping.

A cigar sun leaves behind an ash moon and the soot of a forest night.
A cigar sun with sunrise match and smoke cloud and the smell of lighted leaf.

The reflection at a boundary, the fixed strings of seasons; mass-induced, resistance-loaded breathing.
The reflection at a boundary, the fixed strings of seasons; the forced, the fixed breathing.

An incisional wind with the closure of cloud and rain.
An incisional wind sutured with season, sutured with sound.

Indirect light, shades under tree, under moon, under cloud.
Indirect light, black lung of night, the coal gully and the canal broken locks of emphysema.

Interstitial leaves among the flagpoles of the forest.
Interstitial leaves swimming veined and fibered, with junction rhythm.

The inability to thaw or blossom, the inability to breathe rain or green.
The inability for the frigid, frozen forest to cry.

The river laceration of lake in the flow of forest.
The river laceration rib of water.

Muscle of orbit; white blink, green blink, autumn blink.
Muscle of orbit; forest Sagittarius season and sky identified by the arrow of a steady breathing archer.

String free and stem free, winds accumulate into a ganglion of fall leaves.
String free and stem free, symphony free, the sonata of autumn's accent, autumn's accompaniment.

The clenched jaw of spring, bud-like molars of maples, the trigeminal trees of teeth.
The clenched jaw of winter, breath and bite, a teething thaw of a springtime chewing of snow.

Pang of rain, the twin gestation of lightning and thunder fed by a maternal cloud circulation.
Pang of rain, the navigating nerve, breath sharp and sudden during the birth of storm.

Andrew G. Zubinas

The withdrawal of winter, the strangulated season.
The withdrawal of winter, the collected chills, the trees in tunics of whitlow white.

The wilderness of the innate; the abandoned cottage, the abandoned barn, the abandoned lighthouse.
The wilderness of the innate; the breath response of forest forceps clipped by a wedge of leaf.

Deer and squirrels everywhere; we breathe.
Deer and squirrels everywhere; dreamlike.

Variations in breathing; LITHUANIA, LIETUVA, ЛІТВА, LITWA, ЛИТВА.
Variations in breathing; white lung to black lung.

Tumor forest season measured in weeks and months.
Tumor forest season excised by climate.

Feathers of white cloud, dirty with the commerce of slate and charcoal following the toll-like time.
Feathers of green leaf, the down interior of the labyrinth of lung.

The Gordian knot of pulmonary artery and vein, of Medusa oak root.
The Gordian knot of forest fear, flight, fight, and fright.

Remodeling of the landscape, an insult of frost, an injury of ground glass opacity.
Remodeling of the landscape, an infective wind creates inspiratory leaf crackles.

Organizing, the significant digital clubbing of spring buds.
Organizing, the significant cleverness of a swarm.

First leaf; her small waist, her spine, her breath.
First leaf; idealized in maturity.

Buffered by light; the loading of spring buds, the unloading of fall leaves.
Buffered by light; blood light, blood buds, blood leaves.

The acid leaves of a summer tree's drought, the autumn's leaf=filled grounds.
The acid leaves of a fall tree's red, a fall tree's orange or yellow.

Breaking the whole into parts; Lithuanian "ugnis" for fire, "vanduo" for water, "žemė" for earth.
Breaking the whole into parts; Lithuanian "vėjas" for wind.

Capsules of sun and moon, yellow and white, swallowed into the pharynx of the forest.
Capsules of sun and moon, vapors diffuse and dilute, digested dry and damp.

The angle of this view, sky skin in cyan.
The angle of this view, sun spike or stud as the tooth of day, a nailed horseshoe-shaped skull arch.

Descending from a forest tongue, the thyroid leaf of the trachea tree.
Descending from a forest tongue, a goiter grove in thyroid storm.

The chalky, calcium moonlight written on the blackboard of the night sky.
The chalky, calcium moonlight breath notes in quarter hoots, in halves, in full howls.

In strap and in triangle; a chest cloak, chest cape neck of wood.
In strap and in triangle; a four-sided pyramid made of quarried leaf brick.

A duck's webbed foot, a neck's webbed foot above the rising and falling hills of the woods.
A duck's webbed foot, a tree drinking sunlight from its webbed hands.

The forest apparatus of gland rain, canal rain, sac rain, and duct rain in controlled season.
The forest apparatus of unwholesome lung, flames of leaves, an autumn acuity of reds and oranges.

Autumn, abdominal in leaf cavity, abdominal in leaf ground.
Autumn, abdominal in breathing, a transformed color of movement and muscle.

A green blush of mirth after a storm's intercourse of heaven cloud and earth plant.
A green blush of mirth moistened and flushed with the savor of drying rain.

Of arteries, wind arteries of wood web loom and linen.
Of arteries, light arteries of the sun, bright or dim melting the snow.

Blood current green gusher, a voluminous inner self outdoor outflow.
Blood current green gusher, pines patent with green gust and gall, with background blue bath and balm.

The caseating months of four scattered islands, the season progression or regression.
The caseating months of four scattered islands, the long periods of quiescence.

Of pedicle, of pine, of spine.
Of pedicle, of needle lung fulcrum.

The willow wardrobe, an infant wind tugs at his mother's strands of hair, tree branch strands.
The willow wardrobe, the fireworks of branches, of braids, of strands.

The death of day by the infective organism of night.
The death of day by the respiratory exacerbations of pale bloodletting moonlight.

Forest, functionless; the resting muscle tree without mention of an injury pattern.
Forest, functionless; severely limited stillness, a base trunk excess of stillness.

The iodine evening with the cautery of a surgeon sunset.
The iodine evening saturating over the box elders.

The depth of an ulcer realm of summer ceased forest valley.
The depth of an ulcer realm of autumn abundance, of breath becoming bare.

Coordinated eye of storm, swarm, and swallow.
Coordinated eye of air, a pulmonary pupil lined by lashes.

The brown-bellied tree with its fledglings waiting to be fed.
The brown-bellied bird with a bald barren wing ingesting empty air.

A wooden thorax pierced by a stone dagger of moonlight.
A wooden thorax of carpentry laying the apostle foundation for a dozen stone cathedral ribs.

A re-expansion after rain, after spring, after the low-grade fever of thaw.
A re-expansion of a throat and chest cleared of an isolating winter.

The hand of wind palpating the neck and breast of the woods.
The hand of wind palpating with cold white carpal bone covering snow.

The degrees of a fall rotation, of a cervical leaf stem, of flat fall leaf bones.
The degrees of a fall feel about a spinous brown.

Born in green, a breathing through of the winter's mortality.
Born in green, an autumn then dies jaundiced with unstable, uncertain, and unbearing leaves.

Forest spring life resuscitating war, Lithuanian "kovas" for the month of war.
Forest spring life with a jade facial skeleton, a cushioned ossification of helmet heat.

Base breath stem; the skull base, tree base, and log base of the foramen magnum.
Base breath stem; the language written in an unrecognizable lettered alphabet of light.

Hive lung and hive breath with paper pockets of air.
Hive pinecone with wooden wings captured in cavernous cone, a still and static petal cone.

Forest yelp or squeal, the sonata sounds of animal, insect, bird, and leaves.
Forest yelp or squeal, breath conjured, breath resurrected during the green months.

Both as an ascender and a descender, thorn letter þ of Old English, Gothic, Old Norse, and Icelandic.
Both as an ascender and a descender, the right lobe of lung in runic stone inscriptions.

An internal world of white root in the brain case of black soil.
An internal world inside the jaws of lung, ground jaw muscles of forest air.

The leaf licking wind, the body of the tongue.
The leaf licking wind, the reduced taste of a thornwood winter white.

Lithuanian "plaučiai" for lungs; a plowed pulmonary defense.
Lithuanian "plaučiai" for lungs; the work of breathing in furrows.

"Ona" for Anne, St. Anne's church, a forest of devil brick red, onion dome leaves, and thistle spires.
"Ona" for Anne, the onion dome heart and lungs of the columns of Gediminas in façade.

The young screaming children of fall leaves in the wind as they run along autumn grounds.
The young screaming children disciplined, the prolonged central tendon forest classroom oak lecturing.

The high altitude of a storm cloud lung filled with fluid.
The high-altitude nifedipine noose and nozzle channeling the rain.

Andrew G. Zubinas

An adaptive control of thought; shag bark hickory seed, black walnut, smooth brown acorn or buckeye.
An adaptive control of thought; mind breath rooted in commitment, the architecture of cognition.

The vertebrae of winter, hardest and driest, bone cold and earth white, snow sustained and supported.
The vertebrae of winter, lung house and lung tent, attached, braced, and hung less forest sensation.

Free to distort; the rain and river, the cloud and conifer, the warmth and wind.
Free to distort; the forest inhalation of color, inhalation of bud, inhalation of leaf fall.

The writhing movements of leaves, the vectors of a violent and forceful tempest.
The writhing movements of breath, the wind wriggles in season squirm and struggle.

Breath buried inside the red clay canopy of autumn.
Breath buried under the crimson rubies of an autumn alcohol flush of flora and fauna.

The vascular derangement of fall, single-lung stem sclerosing fall.
The vascular derangement of fall, near syncope and uncomfortable at rest.

The double-lung wooden doors of a brick belfry stump.
The double-lung petals of St. Anne's bells.

Black forest copper eyes, the Kaiser fall leaf ground rings, breath circles under a dark tree trunk pupil.
Black forest silver eyes, the argent deposits of snow, lung heavy with the wealth of winter.

New grown, a wood's infant compressed cheek suckling the spring.
New grown, spring salivary flow of thaw, the watery lung drooling air.

Lung bell with the ball of heart, the clang of sun and moon against a sky dome.
Lung bell with the ball of heart, the whistle of the woods.

As the arteries join, the shoelaces of a pair of muddy lung boots.
As the arteries join, bead, and mold into a vascular footprint of raindrops.

Upon rupturing, the red leaf spills into the jug lung of fall.
Upon rupturing, soil scalp with leaf, cold and clean calvaria tree without leaf.

The intima thickening of a forest trail.
The intima thickening cuff from the sleeve of wind.

Cold mercury leaf fall and fevered silver snow fall.
Cold mercury falling, a slow inactivated state, the rates and rivers and routes of the season of sleep.

Forest-like boulevard in Kaunas, a statue of a dear noble, a dear breadth.
Forest-like boulevard in Kaunas, a statue of a book smuggler, the smuggled breaths on printed ink.

Sunlight in winter, the magnitude is mild with the vascular remodeling of snow sleep.
Sunlight in winter, the resulting limitations of physical activity.

Cloud of tin pest, silver metal turns to a gray powder winter lung snow.
Cloud of tin pest, forest canned, foiled, and roofed by cloud.

Speckled pebbles of air with ensnared stones of wind caught in canopy.
Speckled pebbles of air with the forest delta silt of wind.

Seasons of revolution, motley colors yielding to white, yielding to green, yielding to revolution.
Seasons of revolution, the proletariat leaves breathe about the growing capital tree trunks.

An aspiration of autumn leaves floating on a forest lake.
An aspiration of autumn leaves partially eclipsing the swallowing forest rain.

Trees draped, the window winds creasing the green season.
Trees draped, the closing asthma autumn, an asthma abacus of leaves draped in disorder.

The migrations of the mind, a forest flock of thoughts.
The migrations of the mind, a cold feathered arrow shot toward the warm air.

Sun spinneret, a leaf's middle claw combing the silk of the sun.
Sun spinneret, a net of forest wind, the exhaled rain spun from silk cloud.

The woods revert to green, restoring the tidal, emulsified voice in a fusiform swelling.
The woods revert to green, rib margins lifted, forest nostrils flared, the spring contracting vigorously.

The culprit mechanisms, the loads of pollen following beelines, following the warmth of a hive.
The culprit mechanisms, holes eaten into the leaves, shade stolen, the tombs of cool air open.

The tree-in-bud appearance of the reduced winter penetrance.
The tree-in-bud appearance of solid symbols, solid compensating cough circles of sun and moon uptake.

The golden pneumonia of trees in fall, the ghost lung leaves on the ground.
The golden pneumonia of a forest coming to rest, a discoloration nearly drowned with cold.

Tunnel vision created by the ram's horns of lung torsion and tree torque.
Tunnel vision windpipe mountain eye.

A surrogate end point color comma, the sentence in four seasons.
A surrogate end point color comma, the phrases of exertion.

The visual deficit, an ambulating autumn, blind without leaf.
The visual deficit, a bleak house, the escaped air of autumn.

A green summer harness; the carriage year with the wheels of four seasons.
A green summer harness; summer breath controlled by buggy whip.

The cylindrical trees blood-streaked with the light of dawn.
The cylindrical trees compressed by the tumor heat gigantism of the sun.

Eucharist leaf, green-gloved palm forest hands.
Eucharist leaf, twine tendon breathing church.

Sleuth breathing spider, sneaky without smile.
Sleuth breathing shed of moons above the ryegrass, above the low trees.

The cold, caustic and corrosive; a non-medicinal wintry forest chill.
The cold, caustic and corrosive; snowy fumes and vapors unfeeling, unemotional, and unwelcoming.

The difficult draining listlessness and apathy during winter's impairment.
The difficult draining lung, the silk spigots of winter freezing from the spring warmth.

Synthesis of spring; the guns begin to speak.
Synthesis of spring; the lungs spit stones of hail.

The serologic status, a fall spectrum secreting leaf reservoir.
The serologic status, a sky glow of airways and airflow.

Stiff lungs filled with the transudate of fallen leaves.
Stiff lungs denuded of leaf, trees an edematous and erythematous brown.

The liquid-lined contiguous, bubble-like raindrop cysts after an expanded and compressed storm.
The liquid-lined night sweats in sleeping forest blind-ended airways, in dream-ended airways.

Tree thrombosis, deep and delicate leaf rolling weevil or pine flower weevil or checkered beetle.
Tree thrombosis, deep downstream in plebeian stasis.

A sudden blocking of the retina sun by cloud; in the air, an aggregation plug of unintelligible words.
A sudden blocking of the bullet moon by cloud; in direction of moonlight, a cloud of fat, of oil, of plaque.

A fussy bumblebee, a fussy infant in the hot irritant forest fumes of pollen.
A fussy bumblebee, an emotional display of stinger stuck in temper.

Cleaved by sunlight, out of the lifting fog, the gas is squeezed slowly and silently.
Cleaved by starlight, the miliary tuberculous lesions, embers of a charcoal lung coughing constellation.

Crown-rump length, the sitting tree rib cage height marks.
Crown-rump length, crown-sun and moon-rump, the toe and finger sunlight and moonlight rays.

The voiced sound of a cluster of fall leaves, a tumorlet, a golden-brown coagulation.
The voiced sound of muffling winds, of pine pitch, of a shifting pitch in viscous voice.

In propulsion, in elastic behavior, in forest fidget with the wind.

In propulsion, in season tongue, in blocked wind, trees throated, color coats in tangles and tourniquets.

Snow piles and rock piles, the heaped up and layered atop dense bodies of patchy involvement.

Snow piles and rock piles, a dry cough of the woods.

Fragment from cloud, summer as tumor, basking in the benign.

Fragment from cloud, fragment from tree, fragment from forest.

Cloud central obesity, cumulous thin skin, excessive sweating of rain, a moon forest face of thick trunk.

Cloud central obesity, the rapid weight breathing, a snowballing gland of snowstorm.

The muscle weakness of autumn, the low born rug of leaves.

The muscle weakness of autumn, the ground level diaphragm splashed and splotched with colors.

The ramp of spring, the ramp of isoproterenol, the ramp of dilation, the ramp of mountain ice melt.

The ramp of spring, the delicate capillaries fully saturated and tethered to the tips.

The autumn erythema turns to blister, blister turns to abscess autumn.

The autumn erythema evolution.

"Ūžimas," the Lithuanian noise and sound and breath and theme of Maironis.

"Ūžimas," the Lithuanian forest overrun, overheard, and overwhelmed with the meaning of murmur.

Pine breathing; forest of amlodipine, aranidipine, azelnidipine, barnidipine, and benidipine.

Pine breathing; forest of benzothiazepine.

A constitutional forest storm; lung dew in Klebsiella, Pseudomonas, and Hemophilus influenzae.

A constitutional forest storm; lung dew in Streptococcus, Staphylococcus, Escherichia, and Legionella.

Forest scorch, high fevers with pain.

Forest scorch, high fevers with the skeletal joints of flame and wood.

Forest volume comprising fertile lung soil.
Forest volume comprising familial lung soil.

The solvent of snow; pine green insoluble, maple and ash leaves pour into decay.
The solvent of snow; season tissues of forest, a sentiment metabolism.

Dry mouth of the woods, the lungs turn bitter in the wind.
Dry mouth of the woods, the lungs turn sour in the smoke.

Breathing thump, tree pollen seed, grass pollen seed, ragweed pollen seed.
Breathing thump, spider in long jump, deer in high jump.

Two lung dice, the dead of winter rolled in snake eyes.
Two lung dice, the dead of winter rolled in neoplasm.

Powerful voice of reconciliation, the season breath of black and white, of night and day.
Powerful voice of reconciliation, the season accounted for in dawn-dusk chess movements.

The leaves, unshuffled cards; the red autumn hearts and diamonds of the winds.
The leaves, unshuffled cards; the black earth in club lung and spade lung.

The gust, the wrist, wind-hammered breaths.
The gust, the wrist, wind-wintered thumb, index finger, long and radial half of the ring finger.

The promontory breath of spring, a forest fountain pen leakage of thaw.
The promontory breath wrapped and warped in fracture, winter fracture.

Winter evidenced in the congenital links of a breathing chain.
Winter evidenced in the blues of ice, in the whites of pine, in the browns of snow.

The deficiencies of circulating winds; the forest dry as snake molds of skin and scale.
The deficiencies of circulating winds; sunlight and sunburn breathing pain.

The season of grind; autumn leaves mixed in munch and mangle.
The season of grind; the red and blue diffusion of a water mill lung with the white starch of snow.

Bulb of wind, bulb of breath, wall and floor of forest ear.
Bulb of wind, bulb of breath, labyrinthine lung with an antrum auditorium of air cells.

Four season cloisters of wooden pistons; a green spark in the adiabatic.
Four season cloisters of wooden pistons; breathing in Carnot cycle colors.

A shoulder roll wobble in the wind.
A shoulder roll of log, light, and stone.

Treetop concussion, an underdose of snow following the loss of leaf, the loss of consciousness.
Treetop concussion, a fall brutal brown further retching to blizzard.

Seasons, obliterated, solidified in trunk.
Seasons, obliterated, solidified in a rhyme scheme of airs.

The grumpy grove, the homestead winter intolerant of heat.
The grumpy grove, air taped and padded, the cryptic cold crystalloid.

A season, asymptomatic; a smooth and painless blockage of beauty.
A season, asymptomatic; a fire of life spread smokeless.

Undescended fall leaves, unopened trapdoor, unopened wooden Trojan horse, unopened white.
Undescended fall leaves, breathing amalgam growing febrile and fragile.

Tightly grooved eyebrow buildup of tree root.
Tightly grooved major vessels, bent bellies of wind, all segments superimposed with sunlight.

The woods, string quartet, air fused with the H-shaped pterion pulmonary arteries and veins.
The woods, string quartet, trees taut, the bows of arrow and rain and ribbon.

Autumn's adiposity, Falstaff's excess ingestion of Windsor green, bags overweight in color.
Autumn's adiposity, autumn's ataxia of fatty breathing steps, steps heavy with the hue.

The ceiling effect of black stripe and nest of hornet, wasp, and bee.
The ceiling effect cloud of mixture breathing.

The theatrical voice of a summer lung drama with curtain pulled open in green.
The theatrical voice catch breaths and boggy breaths of summer stagecraft capture and relaxation.

Rebreathe in season with repair, revision, and reconstruction.
Rebreathe in season with repair, revision, or reconstruction.

Autumn in anaphylaxis, autumn antibody in forked end clearance.
Autumn cilia stem storm clearing branches through drop without splash.

A long process, tree limb utricle and saccule, tree limb ampullated and nonampullated.
A long process, tree limb lung crus with color, crus with breath.

Storm as black jaguar, storm as black bear, storm as blackbird.
Storm as black breath, storm as black smoke, storm as black soil.

The white braids of a winter forest; the red and gold braids of a fall forest.
The white braids of a summer moonlight; the brown braids of lungs in expansion, of trees in season.

The collateral ventilation of cutaneous color, the serum sickness of fall.
The collateral ventilation of cutaneous color, the degranulation, the shock, the flush of fall.

Autumn's alley leading to a winter doorstep slab of ice.
Autumn's alley as an airway alley, the sound of leaves in stapedial arch.

Morphometric hair, the dark and straight treeline, the colored clothesline of leaves.
Morphometric moon, an eggshell calcification of a silicotic sky.

Slipping, tripping, and stumbling wind in the ill-defined and unknown forest footpaths.
Slipping, tripping, and stumbling wind in an autumn aftercare of raked leaves.

Forest windfall, a bushel of sunsets, a blood-forming bushel.
Forest windfall, a bushel of snowball white moons, snowball white stones.

Malunion of rain cloud, the stillbirth breath before the storm.
Malunion of rain cloud, a high-energy wound of hesitancy and retention.

Stone wind cloud whetted by the starvation of sleet.
Stone wind cloud mastication of cotton white into armored silver into ebony writing.

The lysis of autumn, breath stopping at a fatal fall.
The lysis of autumn, leaf in long chain, leaf in medium chain, leaf in short chain.

Summertime without crisis, the traits of trees and their expanded marrow spaces.
Summertime without crisis, the traits of breath in forest cog and clog.

Spring preload, autumn afterload, the effective diuresis of increasing moonlight.
Spring preload, summer Oregon Trail lungs heat heavy with covered wagons of sunlight.

Soil sunk tree, the thunderstruck Hudson River School.
Soil sunk tree, forest breath sticky with the paint of dew.

The color of brown bark, cliff and canyon bosom touchstone lines in tan and beige.
The color of brown bark, the color of white cartilage islands of snow.

Wind and light lymphadenopathy; the strand, string, or shaft of malignancy.
Wind and light lymphadenopathy; the knot in rot.

Meadow saffron, the bloodstream dabs and drizzles of colchicine, spring toe in throb.
Meadow saffron, meadow open space of dry and brittle crystal stalk.

The horizontal breathing cloud fibers, cloud muscle moving the skull of the sky.
The horizontal breathing lake fibers, a clear cornea sun dream of glitter, gold, and shine.

An autumn enzyme of cooling light, a leaf color disconnect and mismatch.
An autumn enzyme of cooling light, of light ax, light saw, light hatchet, and light exhalation.

Hereditary breathing Baltic Lithuanian loan words of the Viking, Mongol, Tartar, Latin, and Hebrew.
Hereditary breathing Baltic Lithuanian forest words of the German, Polish, and Russian.

From macule to bullae; spotted salamander, spotted owl, spotted sandpiper.
From macule to bullae; spotted deer, spotted flycatcher, spotted nutcracker, spotted dove.

Tree in tooth ridge, tooth row, and tooth series.
Tree feeding with root, breathing with teeth.

Lithuanian "pūga" for snowstorm; forest breathing before the birth of spring.
Lithuanian "pūga" for snowstorm; solid suppressing snow saccules fall in the absence of audible crying.

Napkin-ring stenosis of a life-threatening forest.
Napkin-ring vanishing vein of night, moon in sickle cell state.

Winter cueing, spring branches; violin-tuning pegs milking music from green gland.
Winter cueing, spring branches; maestro wooden sunlight baton, melodic-shaped gesture breathing.

A round seed, net of the woods, forest court horn or feather.
A round seed, fan circulated, an uproar of season green, season red.

A breathing bouquet of Indian pipes, cardinal flowers, and evening primrose.
A breathing bouquet of Zapyškis church brick rose lung, overventilated Gothic in hypoxic violet lung sky.

Nodal stages of ice lamp or cloud harp or knuckle of ice cloud hand.
Nodal stages in reedy voice, the Capricorn goat horn bronchi hollow and backward curving.

Provocative breathing; a high-heeled forest acting in, acting out, a forest mind perforated like a sieve.
Provocative breathing; autumn in adaptation, treetop trustworthiness driven into discharge.

Occult metastasis, the Lithuanian hill fort burn of the respiratory tract.
Occult metastasis, in suffering forest famine with no sesame seed, dried mushroom, or dark bread.

Trees drown in the season of penalty, the season of fire.
Trees drown in fresh fire tasting of drought.

Pterygoid pine in protrusion, protraction; the open mandible of trunk and branch.
Pterygoid pine in protrusion, protraction; conifer condyle, four muscle seasons chewing the air.

An air column; superior constrictor cloud, middle and inferior muscles below.
An air column; suspended breathing in between the pine pillars and posts.

Four-winged windmill muscles of mastication.
Four-winged forest insect walking and jumping, flying with a small elevation of pressure.

Serene circular series of tree ring, season ring, sun ring, and clock ring.
Serene hyoid midnight, hung in ten with the twelve o'clock white birch ribs below.

Sunrise drug-induced breathing of the unknown, under-treated, and under-recognized woods.
Sunrise drug-induced breathing of the band and belt included leaf colors.

Andrew G. Zubinas

The face of conjoined cloud lungs, the thickened cranial bones of snowdrifts.
The face of conjoined cloud lungs, turbid and viscid snow in epistaxis.

Autumn agenesis, autumn absence, the ascites of autumn.
Autumn agenesis, the nonbreathing state of a bronchus braided in leaf twist and twirl.

The pinpoint lumen of moonlight, the midthorax reflection of snow cartilage plates.
The pinpoint lumen of moonlight, wood moon in mediastinal shift.

Wrinkled pleura, the wrinkled sound of a wrinkled wind.
Wrinkled pleura, the wrinkled voice of a wrinkled wood.

Cuneiform moon, a large opacity in the right lung of the sky.
Cuneiform moon, written in forest phase, time's tracheal rings opening in the sky.

Wet voices of the successive swallows of the seasons.
Wet voices of the leaves in incomplete relaxation, the bronchial atresia of autumn.

Two-thirds tree, tree taste sensation, summer sensation.
Two-thirds tree, the internal acoustic meatus of a wind-=bound wooden purse string.

Eight seasons in echo, the wind-borne time wall of the posterior cranial fossa.
Eight seasons in echo, the wind-borne leaf in autumn color vertigo.

The taste buds of spring, Mother Nature licking the woodlands with light.
The taste buds of spring, the flavored breathing of a chest full of spices.

Vagal roots of a maple tree; voice drops in the soil.
Vagal roots of a maple tree; depressions in the earth, jugular drops of breathing.

Lengthwise peak pressures; a White Cliffs of Dover interpretation of the yellow Vilnius University church.
Lengthwise peak pressures; cliffs and fall's leafless trees in musk.

"Prievarpstė"; Lithuanian distaff crown piece, substernal and subcostal spinning wheel artery and vein.
"Prievarpstė"; forest legs of a winter weaving loom with snow clasps, shafts, pulleys, and rolling pins.

Dysphagia and dysphonia in the throat of a thunderstorm, the frontal baldness of sheet lightning.
Dysphagia and dysphonia of falling leaves, falling dyspnea.

The false ribs and floating ribs of a beehive infested with lobes and lobules of bees.
The false ribs and floating ribs of a forest bend, five untrue forest fingers as the low hand of the lung.

White bark of costal cartilages, the lungs flogged with a bundle of birch twigs.
White bark of costal cartilages, the sternal angle of punished breathing.

Shock, stress, and stricture of storm; the rain-drawn watermelon stomach of the forest.
Shock, stress, and stricture of storm; cloud in gland branching with ulcers and varicies of wind.

Horseshoe lung cloud, hoofs of rain galloping on the forest green.
Horseshoe lung cloud, a rainbow of bridging bronchus.

Valveless trees stand sleeping.
Valveless trees stand sad, a breathing backpressure in the rigid.

An acute chest of the woods in a moonlit chest radiography.
An acute chest of the woods in an enigma of elm, eagle, and earth.

Winter's weakened voice; forest flurry, vocal vestibules and ventricles white in weakness.
Winter's weakened voice; forest true breathing folds whisper winter with wind.

Autumn in abduction, the arytenoids of autumn rotating in the wind.
Autumn in abduction, the laterality of the lungs contracting in colors.

Butterfly breathing; Anise Swallowtail, Two Tailed Tiger Swallowtail, Black Swallowtail.
Butterfly breathing; Pipevine Swallowtail, Zebra Swallowtail, Spicebush Swallowtail.

Idle breathing in winter; circumscribed snow shadow behind the heart of the forest.
Idle breathing in winter; an exclusion of green.

A confluence of clouds, the venous sinuses of an azure brain.
A confluence of trees, the sunlight sinuses of a coral lung filled with forest fathoms.

A collection of clouds, lacrimal sac fluid and air in accumulation.
A collection of trees, thoughts in crumbs of brown sugar and gingerbread.

A woodland approach; the transthoracic trees in the pectoralis petals of a vasoreactive sunrise.
A woodland approach; the formalin forest after a mountain of digoxin dusk.

Air containing cysts in a cloud, lumen in raindrop collapse, malrotating about the forest.
Air containing cysts in a cloud, an outpouching of silver, rain coins tossed about the forest.

Spring in high dose, the repeated doses of forest green.
Spring in high dose, the divided doses of air betwixt strong muscles of insect wings.

Forest edges; nifedipine below, diltiazem above the horizon heartbeat.
Forest edges; nectar breathing at the roadside, trailside, and streamside.

Embryological reflections of a winter wood brought on by spring crying.
Embryological reflections of a winter wood breathing in a foot of subdiaphragmatic snow.

Caterpillar cold of winter, leaf forewings and hindwings of a joint-legged spring, summer, and fall.
Caterpillar cold of winter, forest thick tree tongues and throats coughing up cocoons of snow.

Strut of scapula and clavicle; royal bear in rampant, in statant, in salient, in dormant.
Strut of scapula and clavicle; royal bear in sejant, in sejant erect, in passant, in couchant.

A tunnel clustering of trees, branches in syncytial knots.
A tunnel clustering of amorphous air, a low breath weight summer.

Melting silver stain of snow; thawing bell-shaped foot processes lost.
Melting silver stain of snow; spring winds suction the winter bite of the colloid clouds.

Leaf without mind; the fall of thoughts in derailment, in echo, stopping on the ground in poverty.
Leaf without mind; disconnected ideas, disconnected breaths, ideas and breaths without pressure.

The first rib of Genesis; shortest and most curved, stomach flat with the forest in forceful expiration.

The first rib of Genesis; with tubercle below head and neck, an articulation of only one vertebra as God.

Lithuanian "šaka" for branch, "šachmatai" for chess, Russian "шахматы"; winter board in checkmate.

Lithuanian "šaka" for branch, a wooden piece, a bishop breathing in the diagonal.

Lightning fang cut, the wolf swallow of cloud by the forest.

Lightning fang cut, the stained-glass air windows and niches of an acorn cloud cupula.

Forest capillary, an embolus thrown into spider silk.

Forest capillary, a winter white old infarct of the earth.

Forest crypt abscess buried within the membrane of a melting cloud.

Forest crypt abscess breathing scalloped, scalloped in melting moon.

Tarsus and tibia of tree, dug into the soil of the mind.

Tarsus and tibia of tree, the husky steps of the upper airway seasons.

Plush pterygoid peel of fall; a deep mirror of the masseter moon, the mandible at midnight.

Plush pterygoid peel of fall; the autumn key of winter's open mouth breathing.

Autumn's abnormal involuntary movements, trees in a characterized chorea of cold.

Autumn's abnormal involuntary movements, forest fasciculation, breathing in the neglect.

The distorted sense of a space-occupying moon, molar in pregnancy.

The distorted breathing and distorted twitching of trees, the moon in hyperextension.

Paralytic among the pines, the wind spastic and staggering.

Paralytic among the pines, the weak pulse of an arterial moonlight bruit.

Apnea of autumn; choking spell, the cedars in cessation.

Apnea of autumn; the underpressure of leaf leavings.

Dream drops branding the brain, a sunshower inhalation.

Dream drops with the rapid eye movements of maple leaves in the wind.

An opening duct into the gums of ground; a parotid thaw saw of the snow.
An opening duct into the gums of ground; the forest air sweats from the mucin of the sun.

Forest ciliary shafts of a well-differentiated summer.
Forest ciliary airway invasion of beating wings from bird and insect.

Fall's estrangement, the achievement age of autumn at capacity.
Fall's estrangement, the wooden birthplace rustle of developing dementia.

The broken sugar of honey and a crippling dependence of green.
The broken skin of the woods, sunlight filament slivers in the brown lung.

The malformation of storm cloud; storm struma with a lightning pneumonectomy.
The malformation of storm cloud; distant unfenced thunder, cells of sound in maldeveloped aplasia.

Spatial tears of the battered fall trees, color caught in an orb weaver web.
Spatial tears of a wooden constellation, animate and attained autumn breathing.

Trees like feathers in the sleeping soil, abstracting the feeling of summer.
Trees like feathers in the shift breathing of inanimate intercoastal winds.

The smooth, homogenous pink hyaline membrane petals of infant flowers.
The smooth, heterogenous leaves let their speech fall in the wind.

Provoked tree, the sun in the second person, the moon in the third person.
Provoked tree, the sun in the second breath, the moon in the third breath.

The vocal ligaments of a breeze in violin breath attained from the oaks.
The vocal ligaments of the trees and autumn's inability to sit down or stand still.

Light inadequate, the sloping shoulders of a sunrise and sunset reenactment.
Light inadequate, the sloping shoulders of summer shade precipitating dreams in the dozing haze.

Middle forest vein, stream of hallucination, illusion, and delusion in the dark.
Middle forest vein, stream secreting slumber, the bubble seeds in low flow maneuvers.

A wind-broken man and the digit depressions of God; subclavian vein and artery grooves of a first rib.

A wind-broken man and the digit depressions of God; first rib leaf of subclavius, scalenus, and serratus.

Tree vertebra-covered with ligaments of snow.
Tree vertebra articulating with twelve rib months, twelve rib moons.

Pauses in breathing, autumn's absentmindedness with wind gaps among the trees.
Pauses in breathing, summer's inattention to the harmonica breath of leaves.

Leaf furnished, inserting onto the upper border of the wind harp rib below.
Leaf furnished, grasping the green of essential breathing.

The forest crying exists transiently, a rain of embryologic growth and development.
The forest crying begot by winds, the water jewel low set dimples in the soil.

Forest stride, migration of color crest, mood crest, and breath crest.
Forest stride, an increased wind distance between wooden eyes.

An alloy of autumn; molybdenum moon, stainless beams.
An alloy of autumn; superior orbital fissure sparks in the iron lung dome eye of night.

Factory cloud chocolate emissions, the chocolate cysts on the surface of the forest uterus.
Factory cloud chocolate emissions, the soft palate sugar-coated cough of the woods.

The arthritic voice of autumn; walking distance, the difficulty walking through color sound.
The arthritic voice of autumn; the woods breathing a lack of coordination.

Quadriceps' stonecutter lung of Mount Rushmore; thirteen tendons, bipennate muscle of wheat.
Quadriceps' stonecutter lung of Mount Rushmore; the most difficult to stretch, a teardrop muscle.

The pulmonary venous return of winter, the forest blue vein of sky flowing with a red cold sunset.
The pulmonary venous return of winter, the woods veined in ice, the blood drifts of snow.

Trees in tetany, treetop continuous lock stitch of stillness unwound.
Trees in tetany, newborn winds low in mineral, hysterical in reflex.

The splint effect of the wooden lung timber trunk forest framework.
The splint effect of the bone white columns of the Vilnius cathedral.

Forest washout, the fall ground leaves of venous admixture, a wasted bloodflow.
Forest washout, the out-of-focus trees of an autumn alveolar plateau.

Next breath, a forest wind's long tail knotted or nowed.
Next breath, a forest wind's long tail forked or crossed or coward.

Thrown, tree pulse train; riding wind, saddle wind, straddling wind, obturating wind, air wind.
Thrown, tree pulse train; bullet wind, cancer wind, tumor wind, fat wind, foam wind.

The infections and injuries of cold, the embalmed trees of winter.
The infections and injuries of frozen lungs, white frozen ribs of trees, impressions of the forest chest.

Pines in the paraffin of sunlight, a resin or wax of warmth.
Pines in the paraffin of sunlight, a lung volume high in heat.

The verapamil, the nifedipine, the diltiazem; the first generation of forest leaves.
The verapamil, the nifedipine, the diltiazem; drug-bound cloud, drug-free wind.

The restlessness of the woods, the gross body movements of the leaves, a daytime drowsiness in budge.
The restlessness of the woods, the leaves in angles and in lines.

Behind the sun lens, a retrolental fibroplasia fall, ossification-like oxygen.
Behind the sun lens, a retrolental fibroplasia fall, trees left blind.

Soft summer eardrum, the tensor trees with ribs of sound.
Soft summer palate, the tensor trees sour moonlight white with the darkness of evening.

The mandibular advancement of season speeches, forest breathing color presentation.
The mandibular advancement of season speeches, tree word limbs of facial expression.

Main trunk of fall; a late and leafless inability to close a wooden eye or wrinkle a forest forehead.
Main trunk of fall; an asymmetrical smile after breath bells melt.

Arch of softness, a forest filtered three thorn pronged crown of innominate, carotid, and subclavian.

Arch of softness, the wooden uvula morning, noon, and night in asymmetrical season deviation.

Trees dissecting the air; winds dissecting the clouds.
Trees dissecting the ground; forest dissecting the landscape.

Sensory extinction of winter; sunlight-neglected trees cramp with cold.
Sensory extinction of winter; the white blanket breathing of a sleep stage.

Provoked trepidation of leaves, a brisk reflex of forest droop.
Provoked trepidation of leaves, a sound's loss of height, loss of breath.

A fall nosebleed, the packing of autumn grounds.
A fall nosebleed, gut bleed, or lung bleed of trees in trickle.

The rungs of a ladder and an abyss of autumn atrophy with a wooden muscle tone lost with leaf.
The rungs of a ladder and an abyss of autumn atrophy in breathing hardship.

The Russian ribs of the Golden Ring of Moscow, Golden Horde broken; Vladimir, Suzdal, and Yaroslavl.

The Russian ribs of Rostov Velikiy, Kostroma, Ivanovo, Pereslavl-Zalesskiy, and Sergiyev Posad.

Russian forest breathing balalaika, serving the cold beet soup of history with sprinkles of green onions.

Russian forest in Kremlin, Pushkin, Lenin, Stalin, Yeltsin, and Putin rhyme.

Fall's fatty change of colors, a day in minimal change.
Fall's fatty replacement in brown, a breath in minimal change inconspicuous and inapparent.

The clumsy voice of summer leaves, a sleepy breathing of an afternoon.
The clumsy wind of summer leaves, tender wood feathery sounds in the rest of rebound and rigidity.

Inhaled quicksilver wind, fall's excessive salivation of color, a tree's loosening teeth.
Inhaled quicksilver wind, fall's excessive metallic taste of color, a leaf line on the wood's gum ground.

Autumn antigen, autumn antibody; the memory of color.

Autumn antigen, autumn antibody; the memory of breathing.

Fall asleep, leaf dreaming descent; the trees wake empty, a blanket at bedside.

Fall asleep, leaf breathing descent; forest static lungs rich in silver wind.

Lungs chitin caged, the puddling metal mark eyespots.

Lungs chitin caged, the pudding whites and sulphurs, blues and coppers, the brushfoot butterfly.

The raindrop tympany of the autumn abdomen.

The raindrop anchor sutures of lightning, a laryngeal web of light.

Tree status spring, the forest airway is reestablished.

Tree status spring, the thaw bleeding in the airway.

Butterfly egg of the moon; a single month, stacked months, month clusters.

Butterfly egg of the moon; attached alveolus on anise, fennel, mountain parsley, and parsnip.

Uninvolved lung, the low-rate summer as the lens of the moon thickens.

Uninvolved lung, the token economy of summer recorded with sun speed and moon writing.

A cloud lacks hands; lacking the ink of rain, tree limbs write in listlessness.

A cloud lacks hands; thoughts of washing and bathing in the forest air.

The mature lung and the forest color castes of autumn.

The mature lung and the autumn acceptance of a Brahmin brown door closing.

Oak speech and swallow, the nerve twine in tongue.

Oak speech and swallow, the vines of wind markedly dilated.

Bregma on map, a forest sky proper, the ossified Vilnius cathedral with the greater wing of sphenoid.

Bregma breath, interlocking through the serrated bony seams of roads on the forest town top.

Iron moiety of a clouded lung in snowstorm chainmail.

Iron moiety of a gray cloud with chopped light on leaf.

A leaf shoe filled with raindrop hammertoes.

A leaf shoe smell of leathery green.

Sternum shape state of Illinois, over river and lake, southwest of the French Canadian Quebec forest.
Sternum shape state of Illinois, rib routes of rail and plane wings.

Massive confluent shadows of the depleted iron stores of moonlight.
Massive confluent shadows of evening airway closure, of a poor feeding forest dining on moonlight.

Colored cheeks, color rupture; the hemosiderin-laden leaves of a varicose autumn aneurysm.
Colored cheeks, color rupture; fall's severe pulmonary hemorrhage.

Pneumonia alba, the forest fibrosis of winter.
Pneumonia alba, spirochetes of snow, the smudged trees heavier than normal.

Distal air, the sky breaks, forest echoes fly.
Distal air, distal wood breathing liquid rain.

Trees in parallel; a fall gas petal in the greens, yellows, and reds of an unsuppressed neoplasm.
Trees in parallel; a fall break petal in the bare brown branches of new autumn arteries.

Before the outcry of cloud, the soundless developmental delay.
Before the outcry of cloud, the woods prepared in basal breathing.

Descend voicing of a wood's winter eyelashes.
Descend voicing of a summer chest's insect language typed in sound scrolls of moonlight.

Leaf wrestles leaf in the gymnasium grove.
Leaf wrestles leaf with the sweat of wind.

Woods and winds; strung trigeminal in trees, facial in forest.
Woods and winds; instruments of muscle, feeling, and taste separate on tree tongue tip and root.

Green flame; a tongue wick of winter, a submandibular and sublingual wax thaw.
Green flame; spring spice, the forest smokes with longer and longer days of sunshine.

Green episodes of pain in the trigeminal tempest of forest lip, cheek, and eyelid.
Green episodes of pain with season healed through the alveoli of sun and moon.

A one, a two, treetop in jazz; airway fire of cool shade below.

A one, a two, treetop in jazz; trachea fire of a brass fall saxophone season.

Double-masked with sun and moon, heat sink forest faucet trees drip during autumn.

Double-masked with sun and moon, double-time breathing of spring.

Slow-twitch forest, fast-twitch forest; jog of sun, storm in sprint.

Slow-twitch forest, fast-twitch forest; the moonlight muscle tired breathing of the vagus, a net of leaves.

Central line of trees; a hyperlucent, hyperextended summer.

Central line of trees; a moonlit face, forest foramena of ovale, rotundum, spinosum, and stylomastoid.

Chicago frontier nodule, northwest; the Appalachian Mountain and Cumberland Gap lung extension.

Chicago frontier nodule, northwest; the Daniel Boone Wilderness Road lung ripple.

Inhomogenous shadows, the recurring bouts of rain, the bilirubin bound bark.

Inhomogenous shadows, the bark of split lung resolves, progresses, and recurs in brown obliterans.

Forest sleep debt; paid in the cold colors of red, gold, and white.

Forest sleep debt; summer eyelids green heavy, the woods air heavy.

Mountain lungs scaled by vagus tidal tied ropes.

Mountain lungs of tree, ice, and rock with a saucy air glow.

Thunderstorm thrombolytic, stated amongst the autumn arrhythmia of leaves.

Thunderstorm thrombolytic, a forest specified through the momentum of cloud with wind.

Gustatory distended trees; the gully gulp with the beak-like appearance of achalasia, a roost of pain.

Gustatory distended trees; where the wind rinsed columnar tree hands meet the funnel cloud flatlands.

Yorick eyes; exhumed roots of laughter among the earth orbs lying within seven skull palm plates.

Yorick eyes; a wooden coffin breathing procession lowered in the ptosis of a gravedigger.

"Gintaras," Lithuanian for amber; the legend of Jūratė and Kastytis, a fossil castle of petrified tears.

"Gintaras," Lithuanian for amber; Baltic Sea lung tar, smoke of storm, emotional tearing washed ashore.

Forest segmental wall motion, wind-wrought misalignment of lung vessels.

Forest segmental wall motion, paused breathing in additive reductions.

Storm wind sensitivity radiating in animal scatter.

Storm wind sensitivity gain of smell, gain of silver, gain of silence.

Cranial nerves of lightning in the hypertensive head of the sky.

Cranial nerves of lightning breathing in staccato or sheet, ribbon or rocket, bead or ball.

Extraocular muscle branches with intercostal stretch of moon in rotation.

Extraocular muscle branches with a tree trunk spine, light wind in vision vibration.

Fluid of the myelin moon, cerebrospinal in forest command.

Fluid of the myelin moon, a tea set of trees dripping with olfactory and optic herb breaths.

Six muscles; the two-season half-moon, half-year, half-retina eye rests in green.

Six minds; the lateral rectus evening tow breath of an abducent autumn.

Hollow log skull fists; fingers of stylohyoid, stylomandibular, styloglossus, stylohyoid, stylopharyngeous.

Hollow log skull stumps of sound; forest facial winds of styloid and mastoid ventriloquism rustle.

Nod of day, nod of night; occipital condyles of sunrise and sunset.

Nod of season, nod of breathing; occipital moon tree ring nuchal lines of moonlight.

Autumn accommodation; the hollow pupil of a moonbeam, forest heart light constricting and dilating.

Autumn accommodation; leaves turn, the eyelid evening turns, the breathing globe turns unopposed.

Forest involvement; precipitation of peripneumonia, pleumonia, pneumonitis, pulmonitis, pulmonia.

Forest involvement; storm pulse more or less quick and hard.

Adhesive factors; cloud coalescence through colony and color, cloud pore-forming, season-forming.

Adhesive factors; hit hard, hit early, the green glue of spring's early rescue.

Tree speech impediment, hypoglossal; tongue left raw after the fall of words, leaves, and colors.

Tree speech impediment, fall's brown bronchitis.

Dermatomes of magnetic color; fields, fall shingles, a zoster sting through ganglion bee stripe swarm.

Dermatomes of magnetic breathing; dermatomes of bark roofs built on season dermatome ruins.

Sky fissure, the ophthalmic vein of an evacuated raincloud ghost.

Sky fissure, dawn fissure; an alveolus eyeball sunrise squint, a warmed forest retina of cheek and chin.

Tissue welding of a season, a fusiform forest weld site.

Tissue welding of a breath, autumn analgesic agents pulsed and continuous.

Pale-colored tissue of winter, a ramifying clearance in cold.

Pale-colored tissue of winter, a wooden path shoveled by macrolides and aminoglycosides.

The popcorn effect of spring, the popcorn effect of cancer.

The popcorn effect of breathing, the popcorn effect of a butterfly.

Amniotic fluid of fall; color and cold in obstetric shock, ultimately or rapidly fatal.

Amniotic fluid of fall; an afterbirth of trees in black and dark tobacco color bark.

An atheromatous autumn bleeding into the cholesterol color of winter.

An atheromatous autumn breathing into the collagen chill of winter.

Leaky capillaries of a spring thaw, capillary spaces of the woods cleansed.

Leaky capillaries of a spring thaw, bottleneck pulmonary vessels concentric or weblike.

Raindrop-filled spider web in the greater woods, in the lesser woods, a spider drop in the deep woods.

Raindrop-filled spider web in greater breath, in lesser breath, autumn deep breath of a spider free fall.

Palms of an icon, palms of Mother Nature; a plexus of pines, a pine pyre, a palm pyre of ash.
Palms of an icon, palms of Mother Nature; a plexus of candles with dark smoke, blonde and light smoke.

An autumn forest floor, dry nasal passages; boot and coat and glove and scarf and handkerchief.
An autumn forest floor, dry Sjögren eyes.

Temporal tree petrous part; hollow log foramen lacernum.
Temporal tree petrous sternum stone; the braggart petrous part of a summer storm.

Cold coccygeal autumn in arrest; sacrococcygeal leaves, sacrococcygeal lungs.
Cold coccygeal moon; Lithuanian "bitė" for bee, tail taste breath bitter in an air-cured evening.

Muscle sling sky; diaphragm of dusk or dawn throws sun or moon, lung or heart.
Muscle sling sky; sling of spring, eyeball admiring a green forest skin sweating in the oils of thaw.

Regressive vessels of daylight, evening as the head of a black crow with thief moony eye.
Regressive vessels of a mountain in March, strength breathing in an otherwise normal gland.

Black cap of evening, tree robes of rings; the river speaks as the landscape listens.
Black cap of evening, night black lung in spider eye; the cilia of legs brush their web with a spider hiss.

Raindrop pin-point pupils of a white, gray, and black goose storm cloud in the ambient air.
Raindrop pin-point pupils of a pine needle eye; the elderly pine forest breathes in drip.

Water wheelbarrow of the woods, the rib-like coronal section handles of sunset and sunrise.
Water wheelbarrow of the woods, the floating cloud cooling tower tips with rain.

Forest rose eye muscles, eye petals; days and nights of a summer month's petals, moth muscles of time.
Forest rose-thorned blossom breathing, suction of a red superior oblique summer sunset.

Reexpansion of autumn's aging skin indwelling with colors.
Reexpansion of falltime presbycusis and presbyopia, of fall tree presbycardia and presbylarynx.

Malnourished winter, a lymphatic channel blocking factor frozen in whites and winds.
Malnourished winter, white-bearded noninhaler trees nontender.

Sun fall season, the apneic anesthesia of autumn and papillary fronds of cool air.
Sun fall season, the apneic anesthesia of autumn and thin fingerlike projections of color.

"Šydas," Lithuanian for veil; forest lung snow shell cut-ribbed, transverse, and laced with spindles of ice.
"Šydas," Lithuanian for veil, "skara" for wrap, shawl, or headscarf; white miniature, eared, or false ark.

Tear duct thaw, the lacrimal land with an eyelash of light melting winter-spring.
Tear duct thaw, the lacrimal land and eyebrow clouds crying coughs.

An insect swimming in honey, swimming in the molten miosis of moonlight.
An insect swimming in air, drowned in the forest winds.

Trigeminal tree pitchfork of vascular stage colors, fall's facial asymmetry, St. Anne's balanced spires.
Trigeminal tree trident of winds, chief leaf stacks tree tribe gathered, a venous engorgement ground.

Locksmith of the lung under an oral tree roof of a strawberry forest.
Locksmith of a veil of sleep, double-blind silver-toothed keys of a nonliving moon mirror.

Brought into the forest; a deeply eosinophilic autumn sleep switch.
Brought into the lungs; an autumn's anthrax state of wake, fall flow wind tularemia among trees.

Sunlight passes through the ribs of treetops, a leaf-scaled dragon forest breathes in the sun.
Sunlight passes through the ribs of treetops, treetop serpent tails perfumed green, courtship costumed.

Forest evening face, the zodiac nervous system star ganglions, geniculate and semilunar.
Forest evening face, the Scheherazade sky breathing constellations of stories.

The scrape technique of moonlight; richly decolorized, oil immersed, silver impregnated forest.
The scrape technique of the winds; sky ghost tears and the mild, transient edema of storm clouds.

Exuding from the cut surface of a doughy cloud, a doughy lung double cut.
Exuding from the cut surface of a beefy bark encased tree, a sap drop, a sap filled forest chest.

Forest paresthesia of the upper lip, cheek, and lower eyelid; upper oak, mulberry, and lower valley.

Forest paresthesia of the upper wind, a gravestone storm cloud, lower treetop epitaph.

A green liquor distilled and fermented, leaves move dizzily in the buttermilk beam lard of light.

A green liquor mountain lung ice capped in a lard of snow, lard of numbness, lard of intoxication.

Any site of a febrile forest, the plants in lung fever.

Any site an unspecified foldover muscle bulk of leaves barely breathing.

Externa of lightning, written musical white noise nerve notes from an ear-shaped cloud.

Externa of untendered thunder, echoes in the lung pinna, air wood carving of sound.

Veiled evergreen breathing covering the mountain maxilla and mandible.

Veiled porphyrin breathing freeze change snowfall and snow melt; burn change sun fall and sun melt.

Empty trees of fall; empty hands, empty lungs, empty neoplastic nests.

Empty buds; the forest empty hearing of petal ripples, blossom sounds, and color vertigo.

Patterns of invasion; forest heat of an uprising dawn with bullets of sunlight.

Patterns of invasion; forest heat of an uprising lung with bullets of breathing.

Leaf chest bookmark; third, fourth, and fifth rib page pectoralis minor, transversus thoracis.

Leaf chest bookmark; fleshy serratus slip digitations embrace leaf and rib.

Slitlike apertures among silent trees, forest folding pattern of fall's fenestrae among leaves.

Slitlike apertures among mute trees, forest filtration pattern of fall's feet and fingers among branches.

Traveling cephalad, a single-shock of wind; the slightly upturned pushing margin treetop free border.

Traveling cephalad, a single-shock of wind; the liquid imaging of raincloud afterdischarge.

Night fogging forest, the light source of a laryngeal moon mirror.

Night fogging forest, the selective smallness and shortness of insect noisy breathing.

Past season déjà vu stressed in the hands, feet, head, lips, and jaw of excitatory green, inhibitory white.

Past season déjà vu with a ventilatory loading of past use, elusive to the biopsy of a single point in time.

Season rotundum; fall red cheek, winter lower lip, spring upper lip, summer sun sensation.

Season rotundum; the hole of a season bronchus-like.

White gyri and sulci of a winter cortex, the brain stem compression of an accelerative combining spring.

White gyri and sulci of a winter sponge, the lung stem compression of a season sphere.

Optic chiasm of night, the wood's moon half vision, temporal.

Optic chiasm of night, the wood's breathing winds intersect under a proteolytic and elastolytic moon.

Leaves in lateral rotation, seed descending from the pelvis of a plant.

Leaves in lateral rotation, leaf wings of the stretched lungs of a tree remain in a contracted residuum.

Summer scent and sound steps; warm oval, round, and spinous root steps expressing forest delight.

Summer steps; the cranial fossa of the anterior, middle, and posterior forest.

The lungs are seeded; forest engrossment of a season infection.

The lungs are seeded; wind melancholia, wood melancholia.

An anger outburst, the clouds self-inflate, winds in carryforward and carryback.

An anger outburst, the cystic clouds, tissue imprints of rain on the trees.

Smooth gliding of the lobes, segments, and fissures of the forest.

Smooth gliding of a sky-strewn baked battlefield of clouds.

Among mountain peaks, trees in a just audible whisper; the vibrating tines of a struck tuning fork.

Among mountain peaks, trees in a just audible breathing; bark dark band risings and fallings in the wind.

Effort, inspiratory; common sounds of the woods.
Effort, inspiratory; under drumhead of moon, wind-induced conversational speech of the trees.

Almost airless, the lack of emotional change in winter.
Almost airless, the inability to understand the language of the forest.

Seasons injected slowly among the air columns of ligamentous light.
Seasons injected slowly with time's sensations, reflexes, and fatigability.

Silent, still, slow, and soundless; trees in cord fixation during the reddish thickening of autumn.
Silent, still, slow, and soundless; before the gray lung clouds bring the decease of rain.

Scalp of the woods, the forest forehead cools as the sunset holds its breath.
Scalp of the woods, the forest forehead cools as the shadows hold their breath.

Minstrel moon, brainstem breathing bard, rootlets of moonlight.
Minstrel moon, ripe elixir white bee like nutmeg or hazelnut, like almond or olive.

A wood's breath sound, Lithuanian "nosinė"; a language of dots, hooks, and horns.
A wood's breath sound, Lithuanian "nosinė"; forest letters underscored in leaflet, rootlet, and rivulet.

Eyelid of a deer, a veno-occulsive moon among mud-clot clouds.
Eyelid of a deer, breathing stops below the medulla moon.

Watermarks in the woods, bell drops of rain, forest fraction heard as one-tenth of a bell.
Watermarks in the woods, rainbow respiration.

Elongated wind extends over the coarse dark chromatin trees.
Elongated wind extends and expands and extends.

Forest in fracture, broken branch coats among the widened interspinous gaps.
Forest in fracture, broken branch molt, a self-cleared woodway fractured breathing.

Taste of rain, drizzle of salivation; thread-like lightning lies across a bone cloud mallet handle.
Taste of rain, drizzle of salivation; the facial breathing of the clouds above the black oaks.

Forest fugue; the olfaction tipped breathing of the woods.
Forest fugue; an emerald earthwork in the mortar deafness of the woods.

Andrew G. Zubinas

Waterlogged heart, waterlogged lung; the altered taste of a forest silhouette.
Waterlogged heart, waterlogged lung; the soaked and soiled forest gauze of green.

Distend the season, an inward recoil of lung.
Distend the season, an iris ignition of forest eye color change, of pupillary light.

Gold dust and silver shaving intercourse of forest sunlight and forest moonlight.
Gold sighs of the wood, malleable and ductile in the coal dust of night.

Glassy breathing with the transparent and translucent tree air.
Glassy breathing with a breath bunion in the fabric of a forest foot.

Bark darkens with the rain, forest air sharpens.
Bark darkens with the rain, forest eyelash sharpens.

Sunrise shingle breathes in blister, breaks in burst.
Sunrise shingle spider rash, forest ceiling cloud caught.

Jaw of day, sunset masseter closed.
Jaw of day, steaming sunset soup of the forest.

Forest salivating cloud protrudes and protracts, mandibular condyle bone white cloud.
Forest salivating cloud protrudes and protracts, pterygoid open-mouth breathing.

The anterior belly of a cloud; the venous angle of a blue sky.
The anterior belly of a birch tree; the digestive rings of rain, air, and sunshine swallow.

Spring shirt forest threads, starch white cool air meanders down the throats of trees.
Spring shirt forest threads, fall shirt of wrinkles, fall shirt of smells, the voice button of autumn.

Saprophytic breath of the forest; disseminated dew arranged like the compound eye of an insect.
Saprophytic breath itch; cutaneous dots of dew dust.

Unhurried, the near-normal voice of a summer breeze.
Unhurried, the gentle probing of a summer breeze taproot.

Adherent scar of lightning; storm skin striae.
Adherent root of heel and midfoot; soil fat with air, soil skin in disfigurement.

Ankle deep in the autumn air, the trees begin to ulcer.
Ankle deep in the autumn air, cold cysts and carbuncles, cold corns and calluses.

Trees in nuchal rigidity after the breath closure of fall.
Trees in nuchal rigidity after the acne of autumn vanishes, after beard ground and bald treetop.

Heavy water recanalized through forest rainbow.
Heavy water of the woodway, waterway, airway, and lightway; heavy voice of wolf with stone throat.

Freckles of pollen inhaled in swan cheekbone smile.
Freckles of pollen and the palpable landmarks of Mother Nature's forest facial furrowing.

Hangnail lightning, breathing tufts of cloud feet walk the sky.
Hangnail fishbone cough, hungry bone rumble and rubble of thunder.

Cerebral leaf and a single, midline vein.
Cerebral leaf and sleeping stone, pillow cloud, and flower bed airy thought.

Blackened cloud chums and the chimneysweep of lightning.
Blackened cloud chums and the scrofula of storm soot.

Enamel raindrops; a spring bud neonatal tooth.
Enamel raindrops; wind in spring candle liquid, wind in craze lines and coatings and rind.

Forest birth of float; Aeolus cheeks of sail, a trigeminal knot and net.
Forest birth of float; wind flesh, wind sons, wind gods; son of Hellen, son of Poseidon, son of Hippotes.

A smoker's palate; storm sky space, retropharyngeal; storm sky space, parapharyngeal.
A smoker's palate; Smoky the Bear with hat, with buckle, with jeans, with shovel.

Vocal ligaments of lightning; inlets of thunder among clouds of cartilage.
Vocal ligaments of lightning; air in tension and vibration, air scalded.

Stained air of a birdsong, superficial veins of sound, deep veins of sound.
Stained air of a birdsong, forest cracked air.

Aphthous autumn, an overhung cement of colors.

Aphthous autumn, the decent of breathing in deciduous dimples.

Severe combined; black clouds, fallen leaves, forest lymph nodes of beehives.

Severe combined; forest landscape side of head, an osseous khaki wood.

Leaves in pause, breathing suspended in the trees.

Leaves in pause, an upper body of thoughts and conversation extended into silence.

Elevated corners of the sky; iris and pupil sunshine, orbital fat clouds within turban-like winds.

Elevated corners of the forest; turban-like trees within turban-like sunlight, within turban-like ideas.

Membranes of moonlight; silver impregnation in Steiner, in Dieterle, in Warthin-Starry.

Membranes of moonlight; silver soil, silver ponds, silver stagnant water, silver smear touch preparation.

Breath detached behind a season lens, breath pulled away from autumn's optic pigmented trunk.

Breath detached coin eyes snow blind, ferried over the forest river artery of a dark heart.

A canopy masseter of leaves grinding and digesting the light no longer clenched by clouds.

A canopy masseter of leaves with gland of raindrop indigestibles.

Acid fast sun, summer entrapment of leaves; pressure ulcers of heat and shade.

Acid fast sun, summer entrapment of leaves; rabbit and rodent rockbound.

Trees in angle budding, the day in critical close.

Trees in angle budding, the relapsing and indolent fever of spring.

Surgical salvage puddle; after storm pine poise, position, and posture.

Surgical salvage puddle; stops along the forest flute.

A tree tusk twisted neck; mastoid bud and leaf chin moving toward a bark-covered sternum stump.

A tree tusk twisted neck; shortened, contracting, tilted twisted breathing of tree tone.

Cartilage flaps of leaf underside, a soft diet of wind.

Cartilage flaps and cartilage cuts of snow, white icicle pseudocord and neocord of end expiration.

Fall spring brother and sister of winter and summer parents.
Fall spring brother and sister winds acute.

Spliced spirit, spliced snow; air thaw complement, a deep burrowing in the lungs.
Spliced spirit, spliced snow; snow untied with watery ribbons.

A tree branch, one entire cord, a weak but serviceable spring voice of arytenoid bulbs.
A tree branch, wind scalpel stillness and silence denuded.

Fleshlike shaded region of the forest; pain in masquerade, pain in mimic.
Fleshlike shaded region of the forest; clock pain stopped, the low breathing of shaded time.

Dilated green echo; spring oral fissure, seven movements in zygomaticus major, in zygomaticus minor.
Dilated green echo; two muscle bellies of wind, two muscle bellies of brass branched crossroads.

Wind in storm sculpture; clay added cloud, stone chip raindrops.
Wind in storm sculpture; thunder's toothache, marble cracked tooth lightning.

Autumn wound slough, an oscillating saw; double hooks of gentamicin and clindamycin retraction.
Autumn wound slough, an oscillating saw; double hooks of cefazolin and metronidazole retraction.

Wet skin of night, sunrise pupil of a newborn.
Wet skin of night, sunrise rotary door flap, oiled wood in dew.

Carotid sheath of bark, an oak's alveolus cystic remnant tree ring.
Carotid sheath of bark, tree bone in elevated resorption of season.

Summer completely removed; fall leaf forefoot, fall color midfoot, fall leaf hindfoot.
Summer completely removed; autumn's laminar flow is silent.

Basal turn of moon, of wood path, of bird flight, of autumn's breath.
Basal turn of cochlea cloud, silent sky white, speaking sky silver and gray with consonants.

Wood-rot musical atrophy of rustling leaves, the wind no longer progressive.
Wood-rot musical atrophy of rustling leaves, the habit spasm, the tremor, the tic.

Cerebral hemispheres of seasons, water in the head of the sky.
Cerebral hemispheres of seasons, mind breathing forest in childhood form, in senile form.

Thunder ear gain; sound source, sound sniff, sound shield, sound shadow.
Thunder ear gain; foot plate of a forest stapes, mobile arytenoid of an anchored lightning incus.

A free field, an open space; leaf octave and half-octave, a glottis chink.
A free field, an open space; lung in motion, scissors of wind doubling sound among the trees.

Paralysis of the winds; trees in trauma, trees in tinnitus, trees in torticollis, trees in tardive.
Paralysis of the winds; the hereditary heave of a familial grove.

Oak orofacial, restless voice of torque and tension, torsion and tremor.
Oak orofacial, wind sonnets of the leaves.

Frost among pencil pines, stiff-man trees in wind line shudder.
Frost among pencil pines, sleep excluded.

Thin crib of cloud, sugarless tears of rain, saltless sea of green leaves.
Thin crib of cloud, sucked sunset and sunrise of a mermaid sky, breathless baby breathing.

Infraorbital sky, sinus roof; breath of cloud as a nerve block of sun.
Infraorbital sunset, fibers of light emerging from the foramen of the sun.

The waiter's tip of the treetops and the aghast raindrop shatter.
The waiter's tip of the treetops with sunlight spilled on the ground.

Cloud palate hardens into a salivating storm silver.
Cloud palate hardens into a vase of winds.

Forest sedatives, forest hypnotics.
Forest wind drug, wind pill, wind tablet.

Wind marries tree with a mercurial marriage vow tremor.
Wind marries cloud, wind marries wing, wind marries leaf, breath marries heart.

Spring in thaw cramp; infantile spasms of rain.
Spring in thaw cramp; essential buds, hysterical buds, intention buds, breath buds.

Charlie horse clouds, forest feet unsteadiness.
Charlie horse clouds, the sky's locomotive lungs begin to steam.

Vein of summer without flow, thrombophlebitis trees complicating the warmth.
Vein of summer without flow, hot forest air compressed in season stricture.

Lung lavage of forest washhouse and washcloth cloud.
Lung lavage of sunshine, sunlight sky mariner anchored in the muck of leaves.

Autumn air, an aquarium of acoustics; leaf voice result.
Autumn air, an aquarium of acoustics; leaf keys of senility.

At autumn's end, lack of speech; valve seal of an impeded breathing ground.
At autumn's end, lack of speech; valve head removed, autumn's alaryngeal vacant voicing.

Mother Nature's thirty-one raven eyelashes, July moonstone eyes, moonstone forest nights.
Mother Nature's thirty-one raven breaths, July scythestone harvest, black lung of night moon cut.

A titanic heart and the aortic arch of forest sunrise, forest noon, forest sunset.
A titanic lung and the pharyngeal arch of Pan's six pipes, the palmar arch of Pan's soft pipes.

Forest night sky isolates of seeds and stars, grains and granules.
Forest night sky isolates of sheets and pockets, an owl eye moon.

The technique and tolerance of trees in the nonfilamentous wind.
The technique and tolerance of the hollow organs of the forest.

The hand is dressed, leaf; the hand is suspended, branch.
The hand is lacrimal and salivary with soil; the wind hand airway divides.

Wood wound is closed; season savors, season seeps.
Wood wound is closed; air warmth, refill, and color.

Chest arisen, Mother Nature's ear lightning pierced.
Chest arisen, Mother Nature's cloth covered clouds, a staggard thread of light in a wet blouse of sound.

Raindrop ore pulled from cloud; she sparkling water, he still water.
Raindrop ore pulled from cloud; sun ore, wind ore, breath ore pulled from sky.

Soul lake, moon lake; white-coat wind, glacial milk, glacial flour, glacial silk, glacial silt, glacial sand.
Soul lake, moon lake; white horse, white pass, white flower, white breeze, snow squeezed into blue ice.

Eardrum moon, the voice-sparing malleus of night darkness adjusts its tension.
Eardrum moon, air-hammered howl of a coyote throat arch.

Two trees, a fencing competition.
Two trees, oak throne lungs.

Autumn avalanche breath margins, autumn's angular artery color cut.
Autumn avalanche breath margins, swords of sunlight cool with color.

Numb spring snow, Mother Nature's white slip beneath a dress of green.
Numb spring snow, Mother Nature's labor pains, pregnancy breathing white thaw green.

Forest evening, the low-density breathing of fall, a very-low density sleep.
Forest evening, elevated fasting without daylight.

Summer's upper jaw, a cleft breeze, fall's red upper lip, winter's powdered cheeks.
Summer's upper jaw, moon in midline, intermaxillary incisors of moonlight.

Ink ball of the sun; composing sticks of the forest, wind sunshine stained.
Ink ball of the sun; shoulder slug, sort, and strut.

Fall's pyre pure; branch-chain trees, aromatic autumn's storage.
Fall's pyre pure; fall's volume depletion, fall's fluid breathing, a mineral mind metabolized into color.

Lung cells of the forest, an owl eye inclusion.
Lung cells of the forest, a cytomegalovirus chest, wood smoke flakes of ash.

Autumn's strawberry gallbladder, fall's fundus filled with a winter gallstone.
Autumn's strawberry gallbladder, air sac canopy under rustic stone.

Watchful waiting, a spider's breathing slow and shallow.

Watchful waiting, a spider's cost of breathing counted on an abacus web.

Storm in large fluid shift, forest summer sauna hot and steamy.

Storm in large fluid shift, forest lung bases in uterine gust, the voice volume of split-course lightning.

Sunrise in extracapsular spread, in extracapsular extension.

Sunrise in overcirculation.

Snow fixation sutures of wind.

Snow fixation tacks on bark, snow fixation glue spreads on the ground.

Above the clavicles of the trees; leaf lips brought together, treetops in voice preservation.

Above the clavicles of the trees; lumbering lung broken bow breathing.

Venous jugs of sunrise and sunset; jar chain, jar internal, jar external.

Venous jugs of sunrise and sunset; brain bottled, bust bottled, breathing bottled.

Areolar autumn, the loose free movement of leaves.

Areolar autumn, cool air in the wooden body of the forest.

Fall glands sebaceous, red oils of a color breathing autumn.

Fall glands sebaceous, sunrise bridge over the bluff lines of a sweating treetop forehead.

Sunrise and sunset secretomotor; two parotid capsules, one connective, one fibrous.

Sunrise and sunset secretomotor; breath pass across the face of the sky.

Previous season scaffold, the elastic work in deep lung clearance.

Previous season scaffold, autumn's gold standard of dying leaf in distilled dew.

Water balance of the lung forest, salmon egg showy berry sun.

Water balance of the lung forest, juice from thalli.

Spring in slippage, warm wind inherited.

Spring in slippage, the dry larynx of winter slides into a useful voice.

Inhaled sip of tea rose, of Bourbon rose; forest mind and zigzag bridge.

Inhaled sip of raindrop, an island composition of stainless steel, clear ink on rose petal.

Spark gap of blue jay shadow, ossicular coupling of wings.
Spark gap across the chest of the forest, ossicular bone betwixt fall and spring.

Sunset lower lung, sunrise higher lung, light sticks strike the drum of the forest.
Sunset lower lung, sunrise higher lung, light gold stranded sounds of the day in lung tap.

Cross-staining, cross-reacting fall; autumn in pulsed dye, autumn in gold blot.
Cross-staining, cross-reacting fall; traveling wave, lung wave, emerging to be established.

Routes and risks, routes and patterns; summer in unexplained fever.
Routes and risks, routes and patterns; bilobed lungs of the wood.

Wood split, season split; four-field technique of time's respiratory routes.
Wood split, season split; as the neck fields of the woods turn.

Leaf and limb in vestibular vertigo, a fall ditch of color.
Leaf and limb in vestibular vertigo, the spinning storm inner ear substance of air.

Sunset-gold foot, bear-black foot climbs the vertebral foot of a tree.
Sunset-gold foot, toes typing on a windswept wood ledger.

Season pore; gland moon secretion, gland moon unable to exhale further.
Season pore; doorway drops of full doses in four cycles.

Dead ear of forest leaves, a deaf charity of air.
Dead ear of forest leaves, a deaf relaxation, and a deaf contraction of air muscle.

To gather sticks; to gather torn ligaments after a storm.
To gather sticks; to gather torn design of char, clot, and cloud.

Base and body and block of stump in station.
Base and body and block of breath in departure.

Forest in disruptions; ill-defined thunder after sky cut.
Forest in disruptions; hemiblock hearing, an impulse cut into the trees, cut into the forest chest.

Wind nonrheumatic; leaf lasso of sound, leaf valve voice failure.
Wind nonrheumatic; leaf arrest with wind arrest.

Autumn abandonment in arrest and distress.
Autumn abatement in failure and insufficiency.

Rain shots of fat raindrops; on tumbled tongue of the woods.
Rain shots of fat raindrops; scattergram pain in forest throat and forest chest.

A wood's lamp, fall color breath, and bite trapped like a flea.
A wood's lamp, fall flame darkens then drops from a translucent treetop.

Autumn's affected ear, autumn's aural fullness, an armamentarium.
Autumn's affected ear, the wind turns red with leaves.

Source of wind; source of bleed, source of storm-severed amber acorns.
Source of wind; cottonwood sound trickles, hornbeams and ironwoods clang.

Leaves echo dense, autumn's angiogenic flame.
Leaves echo dense, a tumor blush in breath-hold color.

Cranial vault sky ossified with flat bone cloud.
Cranial vault sky wind coup and countercoup.

Sky time, sky clock midclavicle moonbeam.
Sky time, sky clock stump, the weight of the tumor of time.

Sunset in drop attack.
Sunset in cochlear hydrops, in saccular hydrops, in endolymphatic hydrops, in air hydrops.

Soft sounds of the leaves, a rotary irrigation of wind.
Soft sounds of the leaves, the semicircular sun canal of day.

Dry breathing of dew-dry autumn awareness.
Dry breathing of dew dry leaf dry.

Leaf voice veins pool wind hemorrhage.
Leaf voice veins bridge.

Leathery leaf tip lance.
Leathery leaf tip writes on wind.

Earth embrace, leaf lips; autumn's trees half naked.
Earth embrace, leaf lips; autumn's kiss breathing.

Blue pencil sky; cloud as nature's nipple tip gland gust.
Blue pencil sky; cloud ink inhaled and ingested, rain written on dirt after a leaf edit.

Cloud cheek compressed; cloud masseter unpierced, cloud bandage buccinator pierced.
Cloud cheek compressed; cloud masseter unkept meal of rain and wind.

Summer sialolith dislodged as autumn sours; season of parotid pebble and pearl.
Summer sialolith dislodged as salivary winds carve color.

Re-entrance of the winds, winds drug eluting.
Re-entrance of the winds, a short run.

Life as a bulb; roses yellow to white, roses mauve to pink, roses orange to apricot.
Life as a bulb; roses red, roses bee balm, roses perfume breathe.

Hard wind, hard season; the droplet nuclei of rain.
Hard wind, hard season; the airborne inoculation of the woods.

Leaves rain, timber creek branches.
Leaves rain, timber creek double trunk.

Honey creek and meadow lake, pond life tadpoles under umbrella pines.
Honey creek and meadow lake, an autumn lung stretched rather than grown.

Air cake, cardiogenic conifer with mountain frost and wooden candle.
Air cake, cardiogenic conifer with leaf bread on a spring stove stone slab.

Cyst white, cyst moon, cyst seen through a thyroglossal tree.
Cyst white, cyst moon, cyst air swallowed.

Autumn adherent, white winter snow turns to plaque.
Autumn adhesive, white winter snow melts into the arteries of spring.

Crushed stone, crushed insect, crush injury.
Crushed stone, crushed leaf, crushed petal, crush fragrance of the forest.

Forest bitten by fall, carnivorous colors.
Forest bitten by fall, luscious lungs.

Turgenev's Sportsman's Sketches; a hunter eats, shoots, and leaves.
Turgenev's Sportsman's Sketches; the big breaths and small breaths of Fathers and Sons.

Harvested hormones of summer; excessive sweating.
Harvested hormones of summer; excessive breathing.

Kept moist, wild honey fresh state; summer's hot tub lung.
Kept moist, wild honey fresh state; summer's murmur, gallop, and rub.

Nodule shadow of the moon; dark air, the wind hides.
Nodule shadow of the moon; overt and cryptic.

Red rose hug, wind hug with thorn.
Red rose hug, brandy rose hug, Chablis rose hug.

Sermons in stones, sermons in wind.
Sermons in stones, the ground log-rank.

Stone stare empty, geriatric lung forest empty, autumn empty.
Stone stare empty, tree nest empty, bird leaf longer flight.

Autumn shaken dead, pines purulent with still air.
Autumn shaken dead, coffin of polished dew.

Wide skull sky land, forest thoughts in rain spatter and scatter.
Wide skull sky land, forest clots a breath of the Earth.

Anchor hole of ketoconazole, itraconazole, and fluconazole.
Anchor hole of storm lake, green lake, shell lake, clear lake, bear creek, river falls, and river valley.

Small motion, tree acoustic benefit; gaps of wind progressively larger.
Small motion, tree acoustic benefit; stapes stiff, stapes strut, stapes slippage.

False artery, dead-end forest path.
False artery, moonbeam lung reflection.

Headshake dynamic of the trees; postural stability, postural sway.
Headshake dynamic of the trees; elderberry redwood double dyspnea.

Long bones of trees, early autumn stains faintly.
Long bones of trees, late autumn ghost forms.

Cloud in iron stain, multiple budding of raindrops.
Cloud in iron stain, air magnet broth-based.

Wind strings above the vocal fold of the trees.
Wind strings below the vocal fold of the trees.

Rain multiplex beads on leaf, cloud on sky, breath on glass.
Rain multiplex beads on leaf, the voice of the forest becomes wet.

Fall leaf comet tail; autumn aliquots of magenta red, copper, and gold.
Fall leaf comet tail; kitten tail and duck tail sit on leaf mound, sit on oak moss, sit on forest kelp.

In the woods, a large comet of air.
In the woods, of the woods, from the woods.

Spring summer septum of falx cerebri, fall falx cerebelli.
Spring summer septum of winds swift slow, sweet sour.

Up down lung, up down sun.
Up down lung, the voice-over of past seasons.

Seasons, quarter year isolate to isolate.
Seasons, quarter year swollen cells.

Blunt arrow of summer, storm in low titer.
Blunt arrow of summer, moon as target lesion.

Season nodulocaseous, season fibrocaseous.
Season thick-walled cavity, season thin-walled cavity.

Cloud, no cavity.
Cloud, above the trapezius ridge of trees.

Leaf lung balls of leaf lung bells.
Leaf lung balls of the upside-down leaves.

Noise-free forest, infection-free acoustics.
Noise-free forest, the forest manubrium no longer bends.

Puffy fingers of trees after a rainfall.
Puffy fingers of sunlight, sunlight fractured into spectrum.

Black cloud black bear sky trapped.
Black lung molded over and over.

An elm's esophageal speech, its leaves trapping and holding the air.
An elm's esophageal speech, a voice segment of summer.

Wind in the trumpets of trees.
Wind in the short choppy phrases.

A belt of wind ties blue robe of sky.
A belt of wind ties treetop speech shape.

Forest winter stagehand; nature's lung clasped, nature's lung clenched, nature's lung clamped.
Forest winter stagehand; icicles in interphalangeal drip.

To make wing, spring sky feather follow.
To make wing, autumn air Icarus leaf.

Some clouds never form granules of rain.
Some clouds single-organs.

Sky in brain builds with wind and cloud.
Sky in brain builds with tears.

Speech in tree jargon, summer's over-warmth.
Speech in tree jargon, forest lungs unclosed.

Manifest content as autumn is sanded down.
Manifest content as autumn heart rots, as autumn lung rots.

Closed eyes of winter; canyon snow.

Closed eyes of summer; consonants unstopped, the wind walks through tree-voice puddle.

To collect the rain, lung water of the forest.

To collect the rain, raindrops in forced march.

Bee mind in song, Lithuanian "dainos," Russian Rimsky-Korsakov "Flight of the Bumblebee."

Bee mind in scent, Lithuanian "kvapas," the honey liqueur of "midus" and "krupnikas."

Trees in lateral tilt, trees in front-to-back tilt.

Trees in ocular tilt, wind spectacles magnifying or miniaturizing.

Trees hyperpolarized, air held in a nerve chalice.

Trees hyperpolarized, trees return to their resting position.

Red-shouldered berry, red-shouldered sunset.

Red-shouldered autumn, red-shouldered hawk sky dancing.

Tensions in torr, tree head in hanging position.

Tensions in torr, tree head in tight cluster, in tandem walking.

Piston tongue of fall, slowly emptying autumn alveoli.

Piston tongue of fall, forest fjord of rock and tree.

Autumn's alloplastic maneuvers; dry sun blot between dense dew droplets.

Autumn's autoplastic maneuvers; naked nucleus of the moon.

Running voice of the forest leaves.

Running wind through forest finger branches.

Heavyweight mesh of fall leaves.

Heavyweight mesh on the forest grounds, a silenced lung of trees.

Owl lung shrill and shriek.

Owl lung screech and scream.

Autumn's adient drive, feather tip breathing.

Autumn's avoidant drive, feather base breathing.

Re-expanding woods rewarmed; winter's vocal aging, winter's loss of power.
Re-expanding woods rewarmed; buds bathing green, buds dressing green, buds feeding green.

Forest fasciculations, dysarthria of the day.
Forest fasciculations, forest wind tongue musculature.

Fall leaf bucket drops, capillary color.
Fall leaf bucket drops, a well of winds.

Within the woods, chin cheek cold.
Within the woods, leaf buds within tongue of wind.

The talk of the trees as the forest eats wind.
The talk of the trees with the tonsillar talk of sunrise and sunset.

Moisture performance of rain in symphony.
Moisture performance of storm in splinter hemorrhage, of storm in vascular injury.

Moon crawl as a molding nucleus.
Moon crawl as a scar or stain nucleus, as a shadow or smudge nucleus.

Cloud attacked and abused, the offending ear of a storm cloud.
Cloud attacked and abused, forest anger and ambivalence, both lung fields become blurred.

Fall, autumn's entire lung in apparition.
Fall, autumn's entire lung in extensive denudation.

Drift and shift of the clouds, storm cloud begins to cough and sneeze.
Drift and shift of the trees, long-distance kiss of the wind.

Red leaf patch to plaque proliferation.
Red leaf of maple heart.

Double fovea of hawk eye, of falcon eye, of eagle eye.
Double vision of rain mixed with snow; double breathing making bales of sunshine and moonlight.

Wood leaf elevated eyelid.
Wood leaf elevated breathing, fall clumsiness of leaf descending the stairs of wind.

Tears in thaw, thaw breathing of the woods.
Tears in thaw, the newborn larynx of spring.

Blend mode of fall, leaf pelvic volume of color.
Blend mode of fall, blend breathing in the dew.

Ptosis of the pines with hung fresh air.
Ptosis of the pines under the extraocular muscles of moonlight.

Sky cave, storm cloud stalagmite cricoid ring and vocal cord.
Sky cave, lung cave of the woods.

Lithuanian "juosta," a sash of rain, storm shoulder shrug.
Lithuanian "juosta," a sash of rainbow across forest chest, free treetop threads.

Summer, warm and flushed, sunrise upper face.
Summer, warm and flushed, green leaf lung involvement.

Naked leaf with naked leaf in a duet.
Naked leaf written on with the wind and stapled with sunshine.

Glottal attack of raincloud, cloud cricoid split of light and sound.
Glottal attack of raincloud, cloud breathing voice abused, voice disordered.

Sky skin storm cloud; sky skin eruptions.
Sky skin storm rain released by rupture; inclusion-bearing raindrops.

Stethoscope of the sky, forest leaf stutter and stenosis, stridor and spasm.
Stethoscope of the sky, sky tube drilled tunnel of wind.

Rain, the forest becomes a sunken eye of green.
Rain, the forest becomes a clean sunken lung.

Wet pines petrosal; drip greater, lesser, or deep.
Wet pines petrosal; phalanx pine salivary air becomes lacrimal.

Fall sigh; wind sigh; tree sigh.
Fall sigh; an autumn tree stands denervated, degenerated, degloved, and denuded.

Skeptic of storm, rain cloud less-than-true.
Skeptic of storm, sky without choke or cough.

Wind in the unprotected trees.
Wind in the unprotected ear of the forest.

Finger pressure of rain tears; longer to fill, longer to empty.
Finger pressure of rain tears; as the sky head pain expands outward, as the storm pain resolves.

Fading winds, fading voice of the woods.
Fading winds, fading cerebellar fits of the leaves.

Autumn's angioedema, autumn's bilingualism.
Autumn's angioedema, autumn's airway of color.

Bony erosion of moon, of snow during spring.
Bony erosion of cloud through storm, of white fog through sunshine.

Sky shoe on cobblestone clouds.
Sky shoe on a track of forest wind.

Sky blindfolded by cloud, sky not dark.
Sky blindfolded by cloud, sky blindfold breathing.

Cavitary lung sunset, a red cell cast sunset.
Cavitary lung sunset, sky red bud, sky fallen petal, sky seed casing of evening.

To shed light, to shed leaves, to shed tears, to shed breaths.
To shed light, autumn's adequate level of effect.

Woody skeletons of trees, lung apices in rough and tumble.
Woody skeletons of trees, movement into and out of autumn's chair.

Wanderlust winds, pulmonary signs of the seasons.
Wanderlust winds, to jar pollen in windy places and in windy ways.

Learned optimism of dawn, learned pessimism of dusk.
Learned breathing of the woods.

Forest lung teahouse, autumn leaves the color of simmering tea.
Forest lung teahouse, sky sieve strained rain through cloud tea bag.

Raindrop diamond burr on leaf, rose oil rain from black rose of storm cloud.
Raindrop diamond burr on leaf, rain gem breath jewels on cloud.

Summer glottal fry, summer signs, and symptoms of heat.
Summer glottal fry, summer stillness of the mind, summer progression free.

Scanning speech of the forest wind, balanced bodies of the trees.
Scanning speech of the forest wind, screamer's nodule of howl.

Vascular lung of fall, antler-like branches.
Vascular lung of fall, ground cloth, and ground cover.

Cheek of dense thickets, fall wind chewed leaves of cherry and butterscotch.
Cheek of dense thickets, fall wind chewed leaves with spice bush beneath.

An autumn smile, fall trees left in poor dentition.
An autumn smile, floor of mouth, floor of wood, floor of leaf breath overweight.

Pharyngeal branches; forest branches in the wind.
Pharyngeal branches; above the normal voice of the woods.

Wet respiration beneath the soft palate arch of the sky.
Wet respiration stress strain storm.

Veins and vines of wind, carotid pulse of a spring mind.
Veins and vines of wind, carotid tied tree forest brain.

Field of a wing, fledgling eye covered by wing.
Field of a wing, fledgling and falcon in an alveolar nest.

Sunset lozenge, when the swallow of day is completed.
Sunset lozenge, sunset breath ball, sunset sky strangulation.

Speech stimulant of forest wind, binding or linking wind.
Speech stimulant of forest wind, starlight stimulant of the sky.

As tree stands from voice seat, as tree scapula rotates laterally in the wind.
As tree stands from voice seat, as leaf sits in a stapes wind pull.

Autumn alveolus turns cold, naked vagus of trees.
Autumn alveolus turns cold, season surfactant of frost.

Sky huckleberry, thimbleberry, and salmonberry; sky arytenoid swelling of sunrise and sunset.
Sky huckleberry, thimbleberry, and salmonberry; sky alveolus watered by wind.

Snowfall coagulate negative.
Snowfall caudal crystal, caudal breath.

Tree sway, hypoglossal heights.
Tree sway, breath sway, kiss sway of wind tongue forest tongue.

Sunrise onion begins to boil, sunshine cut, forest frost melts.
Sunrise onion begins to boil, sunshine smell of forest stew.

Molten sun of amber, cloud caught; molten glass of raindrop, insect caught.
Molten sun of amber, molten breath forest mist molded.

Styloid stump sky stump muscle of rain and wind.
Styloid stump on a glossopharyngeal ground.

Moon phase-locked, cyst compressed, cyst collapsed.
Moon phase-locked, cup or crescent bone cement.

Earth after rainfall, earth scored with scars.
Earth after rainfall, air sutureless without dirt.

Presence of stone, behind-the-ear of a rock.
Presence of air, natural to bird.

Clouds cuneiform and corniculate, clouds completely chondrify.
Clouds cuneiform and corniculate, wind waiver in the laryngeal skeleton of a storm cloud.

Toughening of the clouds, uncomfortable breathing of the sky.
Toughening of the clouds, a hair of lightning in the cochlear place of cloud.

Brass sunlight, brass taste of pine palatoglossal, pine palatopharyngeal.
Brass sunlight, brass instrument of air.

In the Lithuanian forest, when birds find food.
In the Lithuanian forest, where one breathes the memory of Trakai castle, church, and cemetery.

Laryngeal inlet of leaves in the treetops, inspiration time.
Laryngeal inlet of leaves in the treetops, expiration time.

Autumn, when candle leaf lights candle leaf.
Autumn, when candle tree blows out.

Veil of web, spider dance arabesque.
Veil of web, mime theater in the wind.

Spider needle, scissor, and knife.
Spider fly caught breathing.

Sunrise tooth, gingivae of the woods.
Sunset tooth, dark soil of air.

Moonbeam thighs, moon arc ballerina curtsey.
Moonbeam thighs, forest night breathing.

Wind building blocks, big leaf maple laryngeal branches.
Wind building blocks, big leaf maple movements of laryngeal joints.

Upper free margin of the trees; spaces or compartments of air.
Upper free margin of the trees; pre-epiglottic, paraglottic, and subglottic spaces of the leaves.

Manner of vocal color; arytenoid tips of the trees, autumn arytenoid, autumn aryepiglottic.
Manner of vocal color; winds work the phonatory task of an adult forest larynx.

Anthill icicles of earth, air mind, and memory of an anthill lung.
Anthill icicles of earth, summer snow drifts of white dandelion seed.

Speech superior to the forest, storm winds in lip-split approach.
Speech superior to the forest, storm winds in lingual release.

Summer becomes sticky, an inadequately ventilated lung of the woods.
Summer becomes sticky, cool cloud cough.

Late fall's loss of appetite, autumn's belly becomes empty.
Late fall's loss of color consciousness, lung bottom filled with forest leaves.

Blind breathing, forest sight loss after sunset.
Blind breathing, blind trees with leaf loss.

As the forest winds mutter and mumble, spring summer pair.
As the forest winds mutter and mumble, spring summer breath builds.

Blush breath, a skin sensation of fall.
Blush breath, a skin autumn aging.

Water leaf, water breath, cloud water exchange.
Water leaf, water breath, soil water uptake.

Decibel difference of rain on leaf, on soil, on stone.
Decibel difference of summer end-inspiration, of winter end-expiration.

The quick stain rain, quicksilver raindrops.
The quick stain rain, quick breathing of the woods.

Wood strawberry in the alveolar corners of the forest.
Wood strawberry in the lower leaves, in the wood-chipped trails.

Stand-alone tree, stone stands alone, stag stands alone.
Stand-alone breath of a forest day, sun stands alone.

Forest fall ground, a lung herniation of leaves.
Forest fall ground, forest petechia and purpura, forest paste and puree.

Autumn ataxic anchors of leaves fall in all directions.
Autumn ataxic anchors of leaves fall into the deep inhale of ground.

Bee writes in honey; honeycomb studies and syntheses, honeycomb synopses and summaries.
Bee writes in honey; bee writes in dance; bee writes in hum; bee writes in air.

Forest peak lung of noon.
Forest peak lung across summer voice types.

Tree left leafless after the red anger of fall.
Tree left breathless after leaf dizziness and disequilibrium.

Mosquito molts, falling leaves sucked into a forest floor.
Mosquito molts, red sunset sucked into a forest evening.

Shortfall, raindrop on leaf becomes raindrop on ground.
Shortfall, bird breathes on branch, glide, bird breathes on ground.

Worm burden carry tree.
Worm burden carry breath burden.

Lingual leaf of lingual branch, utterance length of a loose branch.
Lingual leaf posterior third, epiglottic air net knot of a loose branch.

The ear of wind, cloud bone covering.
The ear of rain, cloud fullness and pressure.

Leaf deaf and dizzy, the autumn breeze.
Leaf deaf and dizzy, the moon mind cerebellopontine angle, cerebellopontine wane.

Summer breeze entrance of air, slight-mild, slight-mind.
Summer breeze entrance of air, the sun's eye is cleaned.

Light-headed white cloud, cartilaginous struts, cartilaginous edges.
Light-headed white cloud, incapable of hiccup.

Spring plants surface into the season, surface into the air.
Spring plants suckle without aspiration.

The day's arising artery, ascending artery of sunshine seepage.
The day's arising artery, ascending artery of sun in the lung dome of sky.

Tree of thought, the wind is driven back and forth.
Tree of thought, a decision tree full of leaves.

Sun in the tricuspid; sunrise, noon, sunset.
Sun in the tricuspid; moon mitral, forest nonrheumatic.

Cool air, prelinguistic autumn.
Cool air, sunset tucked under an evening's black blanket.

Internal sutures, cloud connected cloud.
Internal sutures, wind connected forest connected rustle.

Between the angles of the trees, between the angles of the leaves.
Between the angles of the trees, a cutting burr of breeze.

As the spring skin thickens, a new attachment made.
As the spring skin thickens, forest airway effect of green constriction.

Ink of wind, vapor signature; a spring-young author writes in green.
Ink of wind, vapor signature; a fall-senior author writes in red.

Breeze in, breeze out; a leaf load of listlessness and lethargy.
Breeze in, breeze out; a blunting or cooling of the wood's effect.

Forest leaves like dolphins during fall.
Forest wind like dolphin whistles.

Forest fall in red fill, forest flower in pink fill.
Forest fall with second order cones of pine dislodged and disbursed.

Many snows, many moons; forest bronchiole and bronchus become icy.
Many snows, many moons; mink in a fur of snow.

Vocal doses of wind leaf, vocal loads of leaf wind.
Vocal doses of wind leaf, the laryngeal rotation of the tree.

Autumn's final head turn, wind turn.
Autumn's final head turn, quick spin of leaves.

Forest noon, tonsil kissing of sunrise and sunset.
Forest noon, summer air with no involvement.

Autumn, an older singer's breathing, tree vocal jitter.
Autumn, an older singer's signature song, tree pen of different inks.

Tree bark of nodes, nodules, polyps, cysts, and granuloma.
Tree bark retina of rain, retina of wind.

Tree leg stance, lung stance, walking wind.
Tree leg stance, stance on firm surface.

Violin shell of leaf, ingress of air.
Violin shell of leaf, spring burst, and autumn pluck.

Treetop drift to the eyes, a stimulus train of wind.
Treetop drift reset of a torsional eye.

Speed of bird, speed of insect, speed of falling leaf.
Speed of wind, speed of sunset, speed of season, speed of the forest.

To watch the forest breathe; one eye sun, one eye moon.
To watch the forest breathe; season sight.

Autumn arrays and apertures, an inspiratory dyspnea of acoustic color.
Autumn arrays and apertures, tree tongue tip tilt talk.

Wind bending stiffness, standard trees above the sword ferns.
Wind flexural rigidity, forest eupneic states.

Sore cloud, gray cloud, sky chest pressure increasing.
Sore cloud, gray cloud, the necrosis of a storm.

Tree snow bone coat, winter's dull sternal pain.
Tree snow bone coat, forest movement in melt.

Wind eraser of autumn's leaf colored pencils.
Wind water colors on the autumn ground.

Nonscarring; spring lungs of light, the arrow points of sunshine.
Nonscarring; autumn hair loss of leaves.

The season establishes rapport, a greater breathing.
The season establishes rapport, a greater eye contact of solid color.

Leaf expires, autumn nerve endings reduced in number.
Leaf expires, autumn nerve endings brown.

An uneventful summer, summer silence, summer clarity.
An uneventful breath, forest clear speech.

Of good breast, spring breeze bends leaf love map.
Of good breast, spring walk, spring speak, the infantile amnesia of thaw.

Hurt or harm, storm summation, storm synthesis.
Hurt or harm, storm instrumental aggression in the sky orchestra of air.

Butterfly greater wing color round hole, color oval hole, color spine hole.
Butterfly greater wing trouble opening forest air mind holes.

Soil dusty and dry, tree root branch of the forest fossa floor.
Soil dusty and dry, tree leaves secrete air.

Forest green eye and sky blue eye kiss, Lithuanian "akys" for eye.
Forest green eye and sky blue eye kiss, bedroom eyes of an awakening spring air soil kiss.

Sky spring sunrise, sky autumn sunset, sky circulation of air.
Sky color gold finch, sky color yellow hammer, sky color purple finch, sky color bluebird.

Ciliated sun, central tubule of noon, sunrise sunset doublette.
Ciliated sun, sunbeam lining between the gaps and ruptures of clouds.

Admixed autumn leaves, a dark atelectasis.
Admixed autumn leaves, wind-spiraling strands, wind-whorled strands.

The leaves breathe brittle, autumn's athletics.
The leaves breathe brittle, autumn's cold cannon shrapnel.

Sky asthmatic airways, sky dashed line, sky solid line.
Sky asthmatic airways, autumn blended and bundled.

Andrew G. Zubinas

Sickle knife moon, the wound of wind bleeds with dew.
Sickle knife moon, the wheat of moonlight feeds the forest.

Vertigo tinnitus of the trees, breeze mild to moderate.
Vertigo tinnitus of the rain, gust severe to profound.

Capture the window, cirrhotic cloud thunder lightning ravages.
Capture the window, leaf lung size of sound.

Atrophy of the tail of autumn, contrast no longer trapped.
Atrophy of the tail of autumn, articles of respiration on the forest ground.

Ball or bean, sun or moon, sky dominant mass.
Ball or bean, sun or moon, sky alveolus with time's measurable enhancement.

Sky focal fat, wind heavy with wind lard.
Sky focal fat, cloud weight lifted during the painful percussion of rain.

Spring overdraft, tree tachypnea, tree tachycardia.
Spring overdraft, spring raindrop radius.

Summer underdraft, summer moonlight undertow in the forest sea dew.
Summer underdraft, summer nondescript.

Leaf upper eyelids wink in the wind.
Leaf upper airways ripple rustle.

Spring's burning mouth, burning tongue thaw extinguished.
Spring's burning mouth, burning breath breeze extinguished.

Forest, trees, speech in.
Forest, trees, breathe in.

Dash-dot of snow mask, speech mask of the woods.
Dash-dot of snow mask, silver white forest breathing quarter.

Cry of cricket below nickel-dust stars, moon malaise drowning.
Cry of cricket below nickel-dust stars, forest gulp of chirp.

Forest middle ear mouth air, twig thread bird nest submandibular and sublingual stitch.
Forest middle ear mouth air, parotid ice cracks, spring secretes song.

Passive spilling of the spring, forest dilated and thickened.
Passive spilling of the rain, straight arrows of rain, curved arrows of rain.

Bronchus and bronchiole brick bifurcations of St. Anne's church.
Bronchus and bronchiole brick of autumn's architectural alphabet.

Tall trees, wind leaf forced swim.
Tall trees, wind leaf distress, despair, and depression.

Forest organ of focus, the sun.
Forest organ of focus, wind-generated ideas, leaf intellectual framework.

Ice winter heat killed, spring low dose inhaled.
Ice winter heat killed, spring blood of bloom.

Airborne to fluid borne; soil borne surface, liquid marbles of rain.
Airborne to fluid borne; white ossicle ear cloud crosstalk.

Clean voice, clean air above the dew.
Clean voice, clean soil under the dew.

Around airway walls of the forest, autumn's apical turn.
Around airway walls of the forest, the blind wind cups its hand.

Wind wrapped woods.
Wind wrapped vowel boundary of the leaves.

First-catch raindrop, rain melody during spring.
First-catch raindrop, forest lung window tap.

Summer understanding in quiet, forest breathing sounds quiet.
Summer understanding in quiet, forest airways and arteries of silence.

The moon slightly rounded; moonlight minimal or mild.
The moon slightly rounded; moonlit forest airways, large or small.

Andrew G. Zubinas

Canopy contour or configuration, the growth of leaf loudness.
Canopy contour or configuration, the decay of wind tone.

To sip rustle from leaf, a cup-shaped collection of wind.
To sip rustle from leaf, a comfortable listening of the woods.

Grown trees of the woods, healthy elders.
Grown trees of the woods, a unified airway of the forest.

Floor noise of autumn, the wrinkled paper appearance of the fallen leaves.
Floor noise of autumn, the season sound of forest wind steps.

Woods open low, thaw gurgle and gargle.
Woods open low, thaw giggle and garble.

Unfiltered sunlight warms the dirt.
Unfiltered sunlight swept several times by the wind.

Larynx tilt, the forest recites lines in sunbeam, lines in moonbeam.
Larynx tilt, change stance trees in change stance wind.

Tree singer's stance.
Tree scales of treble leaf and bass wind.

Restaging the spring, winter cold larynx pine poplar prologue.
Restaging the spring, forest actress dressed in wind.

Crisp wind, crisp leaf, brown fat autumn ground.
Crisp wind, crisp leaf, split tone of split leaf like split log.

Bone screw moon monthly turn.
Bone screw moon loosened breath, tightened breath.

Sunset orbital rupture; tree sundown sit stare.
Sunset orbital rupture; tree red orange inhale, yellow gold inhale.

Both bases of sunrise and sunset, an increased vascularity.
Both bases of sunrise and sunset, a shared vision.

Autumn green before ischemic time.
Autumn green before leaf crumple and crunch, before leaf chew and crush.

Sunlight gold spire, sunlight red spire.
Sunlight gold spire, sunlight breast brush heat paint glow on forest canvas.

Sunrise breath set; spring sweat, summer sweat.
Sunrise breath set; autumn sweat, winter sweat.

Blue sky of day, vein harvest cyanotic spell.
Blue sky of day, blue moon of night.

Hind leg of frog; jump breath sunrise sunset, wooden legs of the forest.
Hind leg of frog; jump of turtle moon, jump of crab moon, jump of snail moon.

Simple sounds of the woods; buzzing, cracking, ringing and the like.
Simple sounds of the woods; venous hum vastness of pathways.

Deep organ of the forest, muscular quivering of the leaves.
Deep organ of the forest, muscular tiers of tone.

Birds cross sky, cross sway in wind.
Birds cross sky, cross deep in blue sky soil.

Sky thoughts darken in the wind, cloud mind juncture of white and gray.
Sky thoughts darken in the wind, massively thickened thoughts turn the forest green.

Ventilation is halved, sunrise reunion.
Ventilation is halved, sunset separation.

The woods' excessive ingestion of heat, summer brought to a desired strength.
The woods' excessive ingestion of heat, egg of the sun in a tiny nest of wind.

Autumn's anesthetic depths; leaf numb.
Autumn's anesthetic depths; leaf in light hand wind, leaf in heavy hand wind.

Erosion of the forest cochlea, an intellectual field of silence.
Erosion of the forest cochlea, part of the forest not breathing.

Stretch and flow of wind nests, islands, and cords.
Stretch and flow of wind sheets, strands, and whorled nodules.

Sawtooth sunrise, the enamel dentin dew of the woods.
Sawtooth sunrise, frost air cut by light.

Icicles, denticles of winter, isolated vowels.
Icicles, denticles glass blown.

Breeze mild effort, summer's neutral song.
Breeze mild effort, summer's pleasing voice.

Glottal width between sunrise and sunset.
Glottal width between winter and summer.

Spring syllable trains of bruised snow, of bruised breath.
Spring syllable trains of thaw, a green quick-connect.

The winds crowd, the leaves crowd; autumn's acoustic fovea.
The winds crowd, the leaves crowd; recent weight of autumn's rust, a brown broth of beauty.

Loud lung, bird phrase is the wing.
Loud lung, bird phrase cloud eavesdrops.

Grafted into the ground, tree roots of air.
Grafted into the ground, autumn's vascular steal.

The season becomes bland, thaw dries.
The season becomes bland, winds cease.

Backwoods back breathe.
Backwoods carry ruby-red crown kinglet, backwoods carry sunset.

Flock lung storm clouds in ballistic breathe, in ballismus breathe.
Flock lung storm clouds produce bloom, produce pistol stamen lightning and thunder.

Trapdoor fracture of rain storm, forest water and wind bulk flow.
Trapdoor fracture of rain storm, crack and collapse sky, crack and collapse autumn floor fracture.

Moldy maple bark among dead grasses and leaves.
Moldy maple bark among stone and stone water, among pine and pine brook.

Noon fusion, a central well in the sky.
Noon fusion, vocal fold heat speech.

Heat bone of summer skull and spine.
Heat bone of summer static image.

Four seasons, four vessels.
Four seasons, other forest forms, other wind forms.

Before the autumn woods turn notched, fall's pulsatile tinnitus in rustle.
Before the autumn woods turn notched, fall's leaf cloud moved by wind bulb.

Cloud bone window white, sky bone healing.
Cloud bone window gray, sky spillage into the lungs of the woods.

Distinct angles, woven bone of moonlight through tree tentorial notch.
Distinct angles, woven wind of a thresher's lung of leaves.

Sky anthill, bites of rain from the supratentorial storm.
Sky anthill, bites of rain with wind drawl, with wood drawl.

Tongue blade of the woods, a speech slice of wind bread.
Tongue blade of the woods, a speech smear of jelly jam leaf sound.

Wind fence cloud corral.
Wind fence phonetic decision of the woods.

Spring buildup to summer, a leaf seat in the orchestra hall of the forest.
Spring buildup to summer, the preserved muscle strength.

Design in stone, narrow crevices between the rocks.
Design in air, narrow crevices between the clouds.

A structural privilege, woods near water, the plants gather.
A structural privilege, woods near water, breathing beside.

No longer leaf, no longer breathing.
No longer leaf, autumn tree as stiff image, autumn tree as nonmusician.

Small volume targeted deep, clot strength of cloud.
Small volume targeted deep, raindrop in the woods.

Teardrop length of stay, raindrop embedded in airflow.
Teardrop length of stay, water pain of the woods.

Petals of starlight, stars shy and sensitive in the raw lung of night.
Petals of starlight, the dew of a forest sky.

Leaves eating tears, salivary raindrops, lacrimal raindrops.
Leaves eating tears, clean air storm fire raindrops.

White bread of wind, meat of leaf peppered with raindrops.
White bread of wind, summer wind baked crust and crumb of sound.

Gray cloud, ferric dry, gray thirst of the woods.
Gray cloud, ferrous wet, gray drink of the woods.

Palliative wind, both trunk and leaves shift to the left.
Palliative wind, both trunk and leaves shift to the right.

Spine curvature of leaf, spine curvature of storm, spine curvature of dawn.
Spine curvature of moon, moon belly of dark iron, moon belly in capillary fill.

Good inhale, autumn slightly swollen.
Good inhale, autumn sink of color.

Raindrop forest lung detergent and drip.
Raindrop braille breathe.

Sunrise in sky, forest firefly sleeps.
Sunrise in sky, forest lung change.

Enter capillary of sound; chirplet, leaflet, and rivulet.
Enter capillary of sound; leave capillary of sound.

Leaf divide and sound divide, wind divide and forest divide.
Leaf divide and sound divide, autumn's acoustic architecture of decay.

Spring's spicy nest, tree thigh garter of time.
Spring's spicy nest, spring's clutch of breaths.

Winter snowflake, first arrival; spring bud, first arrival.
Winter snowflake, a solid breathe.

Open pathways, leaning pines.
Open pathways, pines pleuropulmonary.

Double-headed arrows of sunrise sunset.
Double-headed arrows of wind, leaves unpierced.

Plan the approach; spider sits, spider breathe contemplate.
Plan the approach; sunset sits, sunset ponders and puzzles, sunset muses and mulls.

Forest rock step, march, march.
Forest rock step, quick step of the wind.

Spring highly capillarized, gently touched.
Spring highly capillarized, spring snow shrinking lung.

Fall's fibroblastic foci, autumn's acoustic separation.
Fall's fibroblastic foci, autumn's fox paw print of leaves.

Lens of breeze, high bell of leaves.
Lens of gust, deep gong of leaves.

A leafless lung.
A leafless autumn amnesia.

Rustle of leaves sent in an envelope of speech.
Rustle of leaves sent with the wind.

Brief chirp, beak brevity.
Brief chirp, brief breath, birch brevity.

Andrew G. Zubinas

Multinodular seasons in the wooden lung of time.
Multinodular winds of a separate season.

Moonlight beam waist, dark dress star speckled.
Moonlight beam warmth, beam breathe of the perfect negative.

Buttered airways of the woods; a honey pollen.
Buttered airways of the woods; the cedar pollen, the birch pollen, the grass pollen.

Sky skeletal swell, cloud-coated glass of gray.
Sky skeletal swell, traumatic tap, raindrop rank.

Painted wind, color drops from the great vessel of autumn.
Painted wind, color drops as fall black thorn evenings become greater and greater.

Red throat leaves, when leaf unbinds in the wind.
Red throat leaves, when autumn reveals an exanthem.

A persistently elevated green, winter white's broken color, broken breath.
A persistently elevated green, spring's elevated dose of thaw.

Low loss autumn, high loss green.
Low loss autumn, autumn assembled with the wind.

Written tinnitus of the wind, twig to twig tinnitus.
Written tinnitus of the wind, pivot leaf ossicle of the forest.

Summer null finding, summer smile.
Summer null finding, summer breathing overlooked.

Weighted image of sunset, sun forest foot feel.
Weighted image of sunset, weighted image of the cool evening air.

The plain language of summer, wind opening phrase.
The plain language of summer, wind slow motion effect.

Cloud with collapse, sky lung tears open, rips open.
Cloud with collapse, sky lung densely congested.

Angle knife moon, day dead, night breathing.
Angle knife moon, drops of star.

East stone sunrise, west stone sunset, stony brook of day.
East stone inspiration, west stone expiration, stone throw day.

Dabs and drops of rain, dabs and drops of leaves; fall's fixed acid.
Dabs and drops of rain, dabs and drops of leaves; canopy color, breathing canopy compensated.

Autumn apart, wind wide excision.
Autumn apart, window leaf creaky voice ground shut.

The thaw is collected, spring's leaky voice, spring's semitone melt of bird song.
The thaw is collected, wind wet thoughts trickle.

Breath cool, sunset settles into the day's dungeon.
Breath cool, sunset bell metal melting.

Autumn accrues a ligature of wind.
Autumn accrues a ligature of light and leaf.

Wind mixes season and element into a canopy compound of sound.
Wind mixes season and element into a mixed connective.

Silver cloud magnet pocket over ironwood.
Silver cloud magnet pocket lung climb lightning.

Iron lung of sky, clear metal raindrops polish the forest.
Iron lung of sky, spring storm severe persistent.

Sky, her oils; forest, his canvas painted with the wind.
Sky, her moon oils; forest, a body of dew.

Supination of the season, deep dam of color.
Supination of the season, leaf fan of wind, wing fan of wind.

Forest migrainous vertigo of thunderclap thoughts.
Forest migrainous vertigo as the sky air develops pain.

Forest stage, first stage, green stage, the many climbs of a child's memory.
Forest stage, third stage, a vascular tongue of trees left nude among fall winds.

Sole sunset struck by evening black arrow, branching black arrow.
Sole sunset extending directly into the pleura of the horizon.

Raw sunrise, cooked noon, evening ash.
Raw sunrise, forest breath heats.

Forest ice hyalinized, snow resistant to digestion.
Forest ice hyalinized, pathologic voice of winter wind.

Inside the middle ear of the forest, autumn's attic.
Inside the middle ear of the forest, a season's window wanes with the wind.

Greased wind, greased swallow; sunset oral.
Greased wind, greased swallow; sunset pharyngeal.

Pressure readings of the rain; leaves cloud blind.
Pressure readings of the rain; forest breathes in cavities, in craters, in caries.

Deflection and deviation of the wind; season hemorrhage, season perforation.
Deflection and deviation of the wind; a patulous forest.

Moon seed, moon bone in the pharynx of evening.
Mood seed, moon bone unconscious skeletal thought, forest deep sleep inhale.

Fall's friction, flame, and fire.
Fall's frenzy, autumn's apnea of green.

Additional sutures of root, soil semi-solid.
Additional sutures of branch, chest churned canopy.

Protected brushings of the autumn wind, leaf laxity of ligament.
Protected brushings of the autumn wind, leaf swan neck stems in the air.

Fall wind clip low, wind clip high.
Fall wind artery.

Forest wind preamble, the beginning of sound.
Forest wind preamble, voice coil of the woods.

Noise named; fall yellow leaf, green leaf, and red leaf.
Noise named; fall bell of forest vibrates in the wind.

Trees at night, a guild of bats.
Trees at night, a sudden onset of scare and surprise.

Half spaces among the leaves.
Half spaces between season breaths.

Parallelism of the trees, circulation within canopy.
Parallelism of the trees, forest lung becomes hard-walled.

As the air darkens, emerging evening of pine shadow.
As the air darkens, emerging evening of forest black voice.

Chest cello of autumn; resonance red, resonance gold.
Chest cello of autumn; fall plays up to string stem splice.

Enlargement of storm, rib rain expands.
Enlargement of storm, tree top transudate.

Dirty ground bouquet breathe, Lithuanian "gėlė" for flower.
Dirty ground bouquet breathe, the wood's dew dot on curved petal.

Silver flare, old coins of old moons.
Silver flare, old clouds of old winds.

Marrow elements of a storm cloud, the wind and the rain.
Marrow elements of a storm cloud, gray outs and black outs.

Sunset alveolar contours in the cut surface of the horizon.
Sunset alveolar contours in the black pleura of evening.

Old tree rich in rings.
Old tree wider breathing.

Lardaceous leaves, color clefts.
Lardaceous leaves, autumn's amyloid turns.

Crazy paving of rain on leaf.
Crazy paving of coral tree, crazy paving of the wind in the forest.

Silver-positive pleural plaques of clouds against the moon.
Silver-positive pleural plaques of rain against the leaves.

Treetop vagal view, sunrise soft palate rises to hard heat.
Treetop vagal view, sunset hammock of the forest lung.

Forest eye season sphincter cloud bone anchored light.
Forest eye season sphincter sunshine inhale.

Lipomatous leaf soft palate, the treetop hardens with complete loss.
Lipomatous leaf soft palate, the treetop arm arch of the forest lung.

Tree branch five facial, tree branch three trigeminal.
Tree branch ancient map moves in wind, feels in wind.

Baby blankets of bud, blossom, and breeze.
Baby blankets on canopy chair and couch.

Wind through third window, spider spins glass.
Wind through third window, fall's broken glass of leaves.

Labyrinthine fistula of the forest, forest favoring vessels.
Labyrinthine fistula of the forest, a serpentine pattern of sound.

Pulmonary crackles of the forest leaves.
Pulmonary crackles of the all-trans trees.

Sunlight salted by clouds; white clouds, gray clouds, and black clouds.
Sunlight salted by clouds; autumn wind salted by leaves gold-yellow, leaves straw-yellow.

Forest clock of wind, lung clock season time.
Forest clock of wind, lung clock daily time.

Air wood stretched vowel of spring.
Air wood stretched continuous positive.

Cloud spider thunders piano sky with notes of raindrops.
Cloud spider silver eye music wind read.

Air of clarinet canopy and the rain flute fall.
Air of clarinet canopy echoes against the brass sun.

Autumn's advanced age, autumn's amiodarone effect.
Autumn's advanced age, autumn's alkylating agent of time.

The predominantly upper lobe of fall trees.
The predominantly upper lobe of sunrise sensitizing the lung of the sky.

Autumn's aortic knob; a season turns.
Autumn's aortic knob; wooden lung doors open, wooden voice key on string.

Chubby puffer sky; lipid rich and foamy clouds.
Chubby puffer canopy; chubby puffer jaw posture of the leaves.

Autumn airway anastomoses of canopy.
Autumn airway anastomoses of color.

Vagal-sparing treetops, no wind.
Vagal-sparing treetops, summer high-grade green.

Cut wind, en bloc green leaves; leaf hook knife, leaf flex knife, leaf needle knife.
Cut wind, en bloc green leaves; leaf flush knife, leaf hybrid knife, leaf triangle-tip knife.

Subsquamous spring and summer squamous overgrowth.
Subsquamous spring and the trees columnar multiple.

Forest bleed and breath double arrow freeze-thaw.
Forest bleed and breath double arrow storm spectrum of severity.

Woods without dyspnea, spring exertion, winter exclusion.
Woods without dyspnea, metered dose of birdsong.

Andrew G. Zubinas

Soft sutures, snow sutures cover barbed threads of trees.
Soft sutures, snow sutures thicken into the ribs of winter.

Cool breeze collects further, spring secondary pneumonic of dusk dark.
Cool breeze collects further, silver thumbs and fingers of dew play brass sunrise.

Deer fly, spider fur, web thread.
Deer fly, spider fur, dangle dance.

Weathering steel forest of cloud-white iron and cloud-gray iron.
Weathering steel forest of wrought-iron wind and cast-iron rain.

Piano parts of the woods play black trees and white moonlight.
Piano parts of an encased forest lung perform pieces of autumn.

Early lung of spring, bud base excess.
Early lung of spring, forest open appearance.

Free floating pieces of rustle remnants.
Free floating pieces of autumn alveolar septa.

Fall in fenestrations.
Fall in the later pulmonary.

Early pulsed storm cloud, flash lamp-pumped.
Early pulsed spring, burst type thaw, forest reinflated to its original size.

Autumn's first gap, autumn begins a second gap.
Autumn's first gap, autumn begins to overinflate into a desert lung.

A tree's pulmonary scars orderly in rings.
A tree's pulmonary scars buried under bark.

Unfractionated fall; typically patchy.
Unfractionated fall; ischemic airway, ischemic storage, ischemic sight.

Uncrushed air, summer stuffed with heat.
Uncrushed leaves, autumn gold weight ground.

Cavity shave of fall winds, emphysematous spaces of the woods.
Cavity shave of fall winds, ground knife caked with leaves.

Summer somewhat compressible slow-flow.
Summer somewhat compressible breeze.

An evening's epiglottic tilt, an elastic tethering of darkness.
An evening's epiglottic tilt, sunset breath trace or more.

Sexual debut of spring, snow sticky, thaw sweaty.
Sexual debut of spring, an inflating passion of green.

Scarves of leaves warm the wind, warm the woods.
Scarves of leaves tie sound shapes of pinecones, sound shapes of acorns.

Bent branch, bent voice.
Bent branch, bent breath, bent sound.

Summer sheath of green, compressed nerve of wind.
Summer sheath of green, summer sheath of sound.

Imprisoned breathing, a shackled sky of iron.
Imprisoned breathing, a tongue-tied season.

Autumn uncoils with a small drop of leaf.
Autumn uncoils into the lower thoracic.

Open quotient of sunrise, closed quotient of sunset.
Open quotient of sunrise, inspiratory ramp of forest sky.

Sunrise sunset scissor tip control of respiration.
Sunrise sunset scissor tip surgical cross-cut.

Internal intercostal sunlight between the leaves.
Internal intercostal bare branches of fall.

Monitor the movements of the trees, the initiation of respiration.
Monitor the movements of the trees, the intonation contour of the leaves.

Andrew G. Zubinas

Tremolo of the trees, canopy conscious but confused.
Tremolo of the trees, complex circuitry of the winds.

Dawn dusk soft blend alveolar.
Dawn dusk deep horizontal.

Forest candle of green, autumn wax wing flame.
Forest candle of green, winter snow smoke.

Among the airways; among the trees.
Among the airways; the pulsations, the thrills, the bruits.

Autumn air is scrubbed with the falling leaves.
Autumn ground centers of leaves, nodes and nodules of leaves, aggregates and clusters of leaves.

Remember trees, thoughts sway.
Remember trees, sunset dark thoughts.

Across the alveoli, across the autumn.
Across the alveoli, brief bubbles of fire.

Out of the blue, sunshine intention-to-treat.
Out of the blue, calm winds stretch the sunshine.

Aqueous autumn colors mix in the wind.
Aqueous autumn drips and drains leaf.

An overstaged summer, immotile cilia of sunlight.
An overstaged summer, airway generations of green.

Overshooting moonlight white pleura.
Overshooting moonlight white mirror scar.

Four seasons, the four glands of a calcium moon.
Four seasons, the four glands of a swinging heart of winds in the woods.

Ahead of print, a malignant appearing raincloud.
Ahead of print, cloud low surge, cloud trauma surge.

Intensity near, intensity far, the highest thrust of thunder.
Intensity near, intensity far, lexical lightning unmoved by the winds.

Summer oversings with green, calculate the slowness.
Summer oversings with green, calculate the midpoint vocalic noon breath.

Every month the moon calibrates its lips.
Every month the kisses of moonlight blow bright, blow dim.

Vertical whiskers of trees during winter.
Vertical whiskers of trees perpendicular to the airflow.

Autumn's auditory scene of color.
Autumn's auditory scene of wind.

Literation of lightning, sentences buttoned by clouds.
Literation of lightning, the pen of wind, the paper gray.

One raindrop, one harm at a time.
One raindrop, one spectral ripple in the forest air.

After breath bud, before breath break, stems of leaves gothic green.
After breath bud, before breath break, a shouldered summer.

Inner chamber of the woods, inner thigh of tree, inner voice of the leaves.
Inner chamber of the woods, inner winds between the branches.

Across autumn alter, a stained-glass sunset.
Across autumn alter, the wind instruments in a canopy composition.

Absolute piano of the rain, a raindrop repertoire of repetition.
Absolute piano of the rain, cloud key breathe, cloud key strike feed, cloud key broken mirror.

Summer sugars mix in the forest wind.
Summer sugars break in the sunset.

Knot-tying spring with a forced expiration forest forced.
Knot-tying spring before summer's initial relaxation.

Autumn's alveolar color clamp time of tree, clamp force of frost.
Autumn's alveolar color clamp time of tree, a sunrise sunset vascular clamp.

An instrument collision of the summer leaves.
An instrument collision of the forest winds.

Incision and suture of moonlight, white vessel.
Incision and suture of moonlight, bleached breathing in the woods.

In the circulating presence of the winds, the trees gather vowels of leaves.
In the circulating presence of the winds, a branch vowel, a branch sentence, a branch conversation.

In the air above the forest, a vascular target bird migration.
In the air above the forest, a vascular target white lightning suture pull-out.

Autumn evening longer vowel, green leaves begin to speak a second language.
Autumn evening longer vowel, autumn air of paper, colored word drop height.

A whisper island with winds low, with leaves low.
A whisper island of leaves left among the autumn trees.

White oak, white stream, white lung of a bubbly moon.
White oak, white birch, black shadow.

Thirty tongue tree, twenty tongue tree, ten tongue tree, autumn speech slows.
Thirty tongue tree, breathy bright with breathy branch.

Fall's fragile capillary, forest floor fracture camouflage.
Fall's fragile capillary, fall's brittle breathe, tree left without magnet.

Autumn begins to exchange its armor.
Autumn begins to breathe.

The wind work of woodwork, summer's crafted agreement.
The wind work of woodwork, autumn's many turns.

Pine loosing needle, soil stitch.
Pine loosing needle, air loosing sunlight.

Pulmonary bed of sky, sky sex surge storm.
Pulmonary bed of white cloud and white flower, dress well remembered.

The woods breathe out an antlered air.
The woods breathe out an antlered sound of leaves.

Vertical arrows of trees wait for the wind.
Vertical arrows of trees wait without breathing.

Elm element, elm elegant; elm leaf under a marriage-minded moon.
Elm element, elm elegant; elm leaf incoming angle of wind, outgoing angle of wind.

Crumpled water in a crumpled cloud; crumpled air in a crumpled lung.
Crumpled water in a crumpled cloud; leaf sky ceramic crack.

Lung diary of a tree; plaque phrase, plaque poem, plaque prose.
Lung diary of a tree; chapters of circles, circles of characters.

Tightly held in color, an unstirred autumn.
Tightly held in color, a tree's leaves, one hundred hands squeezed by the wind.

Pure voice of oak, a lightly shaded sound.
Pure voice of oak, a gentle rock in the wind.

Autumn basal smear; the gold, red, and orange forest floor.
Autumn basal smear; trees in lung peel following the sunburn of summer.

Layers of sadness, an exhale before the inhale of spring.
Layers of sadness, a weeping willow wears the bracelet of seasons.

Ivory shoulder of night, a night float moon.
Ivory shoulder of night, a breathing moon mirror drops from the ear of evening.

From voice to sight, four corner vowels of the woods.
From voice to sight, season hand opens with one breath.

A body of leaves, a body in a summating potential.
A body of leaves, a body breathing toward the center.

Raindrops fall down the tone holes of a woodwind forest.
Raindrops fall down from a serous sky, a wet voice climbing the trees.

Breath on ground, the fogged heart of the woods.
Breath on ground, the grazing angle of a deer.

Root weigh sunset, a copper deficient sky.
Root weigh sunset, air roots cool.

In the lobes of the forest, sacs of sound.
In the lobes of the forest, a chest tympany, a chest symphony.

Summer written with mushroom tip.
Summer written and bound in breeze.

As the winds flee into outer arms and inner arms of grove.
As the winds flee and leave a sella sky empty of cloud.

Slow sunset blink breathe, evening air becoming wet.
Slow sunset blink breathe, the forest left dark under a macula moon.

Forest remembers fire as autumn amplifies into seizure.
Forest remembers fire as autumn wooden brain breathes burn.

Hearing hatch, spring's scattered sounds.
Hearing hatch, pitch-catch progressive airway of spring.

Warbled tone of trees, warbled woods.
Warbled tone of trees, rippled ribs of rustle.

Trees swing freely to the left and to the right, height and place of both cochleas.
Trees swing freely in reverse travel.

Pre-stretch dawn, prelude pre-stretch.
Pre-stretch dawn, desquamative darkness descending.

Low-noise heartbeats of thunder, cloud chaos of voice.
Low-noise heartbeats of thunder, ceiling tiles of sky lit by wind.

Vowels gather on ground, each utterance of autumn.
Vowels gather on ground, well visualized vowels, unlocking lung left silent.

Summer sorrow dries, simple wind touches the pinna of pine.
Summer sorrow dries, simple smile.

Deep-seated air of the woods, thorax throne trees.
Deep-seated air of the woods, cloud crown.

Pine wind needle-to-nerve.
Pine wind cry.

Parachute sutures of lowering leaves, of lowering lungs.
Parachute sutures of leaf word fall, of leaf word foil.

Memory array of autumn, memory mixed octave of the winds.
Memory array of autumn, tumble thoughts of the trees.

Tree toes up, tree toes down, tree toe rotations.
Tree toes in a summer sandal walking on the wind.

Soft coal evening wood turn hard-coal night, a small amount of quartz in the sky.
Soft coal evening wood turn hard-coal night, the sky manufactures mirrors.

The wood's dry ticklish throat, summer's inhalational burn.
The wood's dry ticklish throat, leaf present in the dust.

Sky sparks of scale from the dark center of clouds.
Sky sparks of scale beneath the polished pleura of silver.

The forest drinks echoes, a prolonged intake.
The forest drinks echoes, an old healed rustle.

Autumn slight vocal, color found after the inspection of the lungs.
Autumn slight vocal, little altered.

Autumn's ashing lung, leaves of fall freshly fractured.
Autumn's ashing lung, the ground leaves a collective unconscious.

Andrew G. Zubinas

Canopy ear placed on chest trunk of tree.
Canopy ear and sublight shade dark sounds.

Early gold weight of autumn, a magnetic bulk.
Early gold weight of autumn, wind cold cut and clip canopy coin.

Downblended, moist air of the woods.
Downblended, spring suggestive, the recognition is strong.

Trees ask sky for sunlight, summer forest fully educated.
Trees ask sky for sunlight, tree leaves return thank-you with the wind.

Decay arrows of autumn leaves, decay arrows of sunlight.
Decay arrows of autumn leaves, fall's flail chest.

Forest mesentery of moonlight, the forest digests darkness.
Forest mesentery of moonlight, scaffolds of silence, the bright bronchioles breathe.

Ferruginous fall, cleavage fragments of leaves.
Ferruginous fall, canopy cremation on the autumn ground.

White asbestos clouds, blue asbestos sky.
White asbestos clouds, pearling as they grow.

Four voice tree ring, bubble bark of wooden air.
Four voice tree ring, sutures encircle a firm wrap tree tie-down.

Overhang eggshell canopy, autumn's adhesive drapes stick to the wind.
Overhang eggshell cloud darkens and thickens with thunder.

Tree tongue trills, leaf lip trills.
Tree tongue trills, the voice mask of the forest wears wind.

Wind rubs leaf; forest fricatives of canopy climax.
Wind rubs leaf; tree touch tremble, twitch, twist, and turn.

As air ages, as rainclouds float prepulse.
As air ages, as rainclouds autumn rainfall.

Normal window of the moon, osseous screws of a day by day patching window.
Normal window of the moon, sky alveolus of light.

Summer sorrow dries, simple wind touches the pinna of pine.
Summer sorrow dries, simple smile.

Tip cell cloud partially carves the sky.
Tip cell cloud and a pen of clean air.

Sky sharp bladed with rain, raindrop half tap, raindrop full tap.
Sky sharp bladed with rain, forest vein clad clouds breathing forcefully.

Spring senses the tone, summer tone is louder.
Spring senses the tone, summer surge of wind.

Fixation and fricative of fall.
Fixation and fricative of wind.

The sky begins to breathe bleach, the clouds form.
The sky begins to breathe bleach, sky corners and ends in darkened dirt.

Ivory coverlet cloud, the rain release.
Ivory coverlet cloud, breath brush on.

Branch breathes down sweep, the branch breathes upsweep, swept tone of the leaves.
Branch breathes blurry.

Sky steam ready, blue background.
Sky steam ready, breathe background.

Sky breathing bend, breathing stretch, vagal low clouds, vagal high clouds.
Sky breathing bend, breathing stretch, vagal low treetop, vagal high treetop.

Leaf pleural penetrates, core sunlight, core moonlight.
Leaf pleural penetrates, shown to reach sun, shown to reach moon.

One season, the moon massages the forest.
One season, one natural lung; four seasons, forest clover of air.

Winter uncoated, winter rapidly cleared, thaw reaching the pleura of pine.
Winter uncoated, spring's body burden of burden being.

Summer dry lung, summer dust overload.
Summer dry lung, light burden, the world's mining and milling of sunshine.

Groups of pines, groups of postures.
Groups of pines, slumped position of the pines in the wind.

Turning depth of the leaves, autumn angle array.
Turning depth of the leaves, inverse horn autumn air solid.

A sky shampoo of blue, remove handle, remove heaven from rain.
A sky shampoo of blue, canopy calm, forest rest and breathe.

A road of wind through a road of pines.
A road of wind pine paved.

Treetop head of stillness; circle, circle.
Treetop head of wind song swirling greater and greater into a straight rustle curved violin body
of trees.

Tilestone throne of cloud, gray washes green, wet weight of the woods.
Tilestone throne of cloud, breath weight of the sky.

Sky throws rain, forest catches its breath in branch.
Sky throws rain, forest throws air.

Light takes the trees, present wind, absent wind.
Light takes the trees, upstream wind, downstream wind.

Sky sugar tong, sky scapholunate, moon mixed with marrow.
Sky sugar tong, sky scapholunate, moon peripheral upper, forest central lower.

Simple shift, simple scale, a one-third-octave autumn.
Simple shift, simple scale, simple sooth, and heal of the forest wind.

Common thought of cloud.
Common thought of wind escalating leaves.

Piano roll rustle, old voice autumn tree top, a bronze heavy with the eggs of sound.
Piano roll rustle, leaves of the tree branches break and boom, burst and breathe.

The tanning or bronzing of the fall trees, leaves begin below-elbow.
The tanning or bronzing of the fall trees, fall in wind, a canopy complex of tears.

Sky becomes breathable bedding, sky becomes bed bound.
Sky becomes bathwater, the wash water woods.

Release lock, the leaves breathe open.
Release lock, rain of sound, rain step here.

Disappearing dirt pieces, score and sound and symphony of wind.
Disappearing dirt pieces, rain, the dirt peace of the woods.

Screws of sky, countersunk cloud, windsunk water.
Screws of sky, the wind locking nails of trees.

Autumn branch forearm fixation of color.
Autumn branch breath breakage.

Fall's scissors of wind, tree lends leaf to ground, ground gentle instruments.
Fall's scissors of wind, fall's full tap of thread, invisible thread.

Full face of fall, the puffed cheeks of autumn.
Full face of fall, a vascular view, a vascular wind.

Sky scrub, cloud clean towel.
Sky scrub, rain bubble breaths popped by forest trees.

Parcels of air reaching overhead, cloud called the cloth, sky peppered with flashes.
Parcels of air reaching overhead, cloud called the cloth, forest peppered with rain.

Autumn cleansing the lungs of leaves.
Autumn cleansing the mixed dust of color leaves.

Wooden mallet of spring.
Wooden mallet pulls air deep.

Championed cleansing, sky shoulders hunch forward before the storm.
Championed cleansing, championed breathing of the forest.

Wind whims of the woods.
Wind whims of the wash.

Forest fresh and clear headed after the rain.
Forest fresh after the inhalation.

Summer hot hips and heels.
Summer hot shifts in breathing.

Unrefined oil of rustle.
Unrefined oil of wind.

Rustle roughness, roughness of the sea of sound.
Rustle roughness, the breath retention of forest echo.

The lower airways, an ant facing the ceiling of canopy, sugar and wine cravings.
The lower airways, an ant putting pencil to paper with soil.

Hitchpin whipstitch wind.
Hitchpin pine.

Adding bulk of leaves, adding bulk of breath.
Adding bulk of leaves, canopy clicks and noise.

Breath moving moon maker of keyboard.
Breath moving trees.

Leaf links each hammer, a pinch of salt sound.
Leaf links each hammer, root down wind.

Must hear moon, must hear trees.
Must hear winds, must hear heart sounds of the woods.

Wind floss, trees of teeth.
Wind floss, wind watch breath.

Hammer lever leaf player press pivot shift.
Hammer lever leaf loud and soft.

The final tone of autumn, tree in piano propel, piano possible.
The final tone of autumn, the wind notes stop.

Quiet the breath, pianoforte silence of an upright piano tree.
Quiet the breath, sunset softness and glow, sunset smiling eye.

Moonlight elbow of evening reflected on leaf, bow and garment of wooden violin.
Moonlight elbow of evening on tree table of thought; stars, light of lymph, moon, breast of breath.

Pine air, pine pen paint.
Pine air, the particulates of perfect.

Wood bridge white.
Wood bridge wind.

Sky pump coffee, coffee drops.
Sky pump coffee, coffee clouds in air.

Wind stiff, wind straight, stem full of leaves.
Wind stiff, wind straight, many leaves, many moves.

Speak wind, speak sun, speak spice.
Speak wind, a forest ear of leaves.

Forest breathes bikini with flower petal.
Forest breathes better in summer sun.

Forest fingernails of leaves with dew, rain, and thaw.
Forest fingernails of leaves scratch the wind.

Leaf rain, scour man hue water.
Leaf rain, scrub woman hue wind.

Wild sugar cane clouds, tree taste gray, tree taste black.
Wild sugar cane clouds, wild wind of rum rain drop, dangle, and drench.

Andrew G. Zubinas

Leaves snap sound, sky snaps storm, thaw snaps spring.
Leaves snap sound, wind snaps sea of forest air, sea of forest movement, sea of forest wave.

Nectar of sun, nectar of sky, nectar of cloud.
Nectar of sun, nectar of sound, forest leaf nectar of wind whip and weep.

The burning music of autumn, leaves in dolphin dream dance dip.
The burning music of autumn, the air cools and cools and cools.

Warm air, shade, cold air.
Warm air, cloud, cold air.

Tree rings as seashell, tree tower of Babel, the shell sound of wind treetop tongue.
Tree rings as seashell, season sounds of round moon and round sun.

Tree rings, the many wedding rings of time.
Tree rings, the many wedding winds of hot and cold.

Autumn accountant counts acorns, autumn accountant counts leaves, autumn accountant counts loss.
Autumn accountant counts acorns, autumn accountant air.

Two breaths of thin oaks.
Two breaths of whisky wind.

Forest estate of ear, sandal of sound, a rejuvenated rustle.
Forest estate of ear, sound air carved in spiral, in square, in diamond.

Forest mirror with a wooden frame.
Forest mirror wind elements.

Wooden posts, bed posts.
Wooden posts, wind posts.

Wooden dresser knob and handle, the clothes of breathing.
Wooden dresser knob and handle, forest knob and handle oak, wooden window open.

Leaf standing, leaf while seated on soil.
Leaf standing, a vest of wind.

Billiard breathing, cue cloud.
Billiard breathing, cue stick wood, autumn breaks.

The old literature of leaves leave tree, fall on grammatical ground.
The old literature of leaves wind written in color, code, and correspondence.

Cloud creak vocal, canopy creak vocal.
Cloud creak vocal, four seasons, the flow of four fluids.

Dark discoloration dusk, dark breathing woods.
Dark discoloration dusk, breath light evening embers of starlight and moonlight.

Mesh and suture of leaves, mesh and suture of wind.
Mesh and suture of leaves, mesh and suture of moon, mesh and suture of summer.

Summer suture placement of breeze.
Summer suture placement of peace.

Polis of pines, a white statue of wind.
Polis of pines, leaf and fern fan over the stone breeze of breast.

Rustle regal of the shattered old age of fall.
Rustle regal breathing.

Grove glib with leaves.
Grove glib ground held breath.

Rain down, leaves down, fall's dismissed notes.
Rain down, leaves down, tree drapes down, autumn accepted scales in deep, deep breath.

Autumn's well-aged wine of leaves.
Autumn's well-aged wind, breath belly laugh.

Lung stir of the leaves, stir of spring, forest moon manners of breathing.
Lung stir of the leaves, all-cause canopy.

Freshened ends of leaves, freshened forest.
Freshened ends of leaves, freshened air, freshened fall positive sharp.

Still clean, soft clean, self clean of the topsy turvey trees.
Still clean, clean compression of straight rib trees.

Spring sleep, a season of suppress sleep.
Spring sleep, lungs lead-in leaf.

A long segment of wind in the woods, a short segment of sound.
A long segment of wind in the woods, lung lines, leaf lines of sound settlement.

Leaves and wind in a linear mixed.
Leaves and wind sound stable.

Pain diary of rain, forest rain.
Pain diary evening exercise exhalation.

Shuffled shoulder, a deck of leaves.
Shuffled shoulder, shunt leaves of breeze.

Wedding ring of wind, lifelong suture, slippage of four hands, four seasons.
Wedding ring of wind, tree sways right, tree sways left, tree sways second look.

Bed sheets of moonlight, forest evening eyebrows raised.
Bed sheets of moonlight, forest air absent with sound.

Sucked gums of ground, autumn ground.
Sucked gums of grove, gum wind of grove.

The along path of pines.
The along path of wind, leaves laying stress.

Canopy, a collection of muscles and tendons.
Canopy, a collection of color wind color.

Sieve pine pulse of primer and probe wind.
Sieve pine pulse needles dangle dancing to debilitate.

Wind chelates tree into rustle.
Wind chelates cloud chain gray, chelates cloud chain black, forest green.

Forest hearing four, hearing seasons bundle breathe.
Forest hearing four, trees thread-and-pull sun smooth scroll, moon smooth scroll.

Clever canopy, clever color, the irresistible songs of the wind.
Clever canopy, clever color, the forest falls into embarrassment.

Path of clouds, sky lung of stones.
Path of clouds, oath sworn storm.

Exit and entrance and extras of the evening wind in the forest.
Exit and entrance and extras of autumn.

Autumn's acoustic sink, leaf wash in wind drops, soundwash in wind drops.
Autumn's acoustic sink, thought together tree together songs.

Autumn's acoustic absorb, the create centers of curve.
Autumn's acoustic absorb, late winds, autumn's avoid.

Tree might of a peaky spring.
Tree might, breath might.

Tourniquet shift length sound leaves, tourniquet tight tree.
Tourniquet shift length sound leaves, scheduled sounds of an unscheduled wind.

Winter in a well-defined white.
Winter in a well of wind.

Sky cloud coatings, blue buffer, cloud cough, and gag of storm.
Sky cloud coatings, blue buffer, bulky nodes of the wind.

Sky shows single, sky shows couple, sky shows storm.
Sky shows single, sky sandal to scandal exhalation.

Moon muscle music strength, airway and plug of the forest.
Moon muscle as assessed by means of a scratch of moonlight.

Leaflet angle, lung angle of autumn.
Leaflet angle, the full text of rustling leaves.

Curved rib, curved rainbow, curved bow with straight arrow of tree, curved hip heights of the forest.
Curved rib, woman wind of the woods.

One-hand piano, two-hand piano, purr of the pines.
One-hand piano, two-hand piano, forest fingers in the wind.

Sunset vocal downtime, moon mapped negative night.
Sunset vocal downtime, moon mapped air, air mapped woods.

Air of pine pristine, pristine poor.
Air of pine procurement, proper procurement.

Stream of moonlight in the woods, stream silence.
Stream of moonlight in the woods, stream breathe.

Trees think less, the autumn ground feels more.
Trees think less, the forest breathing dirty leaves.

Forest breathing the medium of the psychic pines.
Forest breathing the medium of the crystal light.

Forest bed, healing heard.
Forest bed, breathing heard.

Pine place, pine place of breathing.
Pine place, pine place of healing.

Meditation further forest; summer silence, summer simply slow, summer surrender breathing.
Meditation further forest; heart text heat creates greater, creates greater voice.

Trees in transchannel, sacred sound, sacred geometry, sacred soul of the woods.
Trees in transchannel, inner and outer, wind builder of bridge and belief.

Within the wind, within the writings.
Within the wind, perched lungs of tree.

Jawline of leaves unwind in the wind.
Jawline of leaves hear hawk send.

No color, winter off-white hoarfrost.
No color, the forest breathes soft snowflake.

Forest faucet on, summer; forest faucet off, winter.
Forest faucet with breath down drain, down sink of seasons, down sink of sounds.

Salt is known in sky; steam, steam brush white to gray.
Salt is known in sky; salt cave, sea bed, salt breath above forest.

Symbol sky, modified forest.
Symbol sky, modified breathing.

Sunset salt tea light; night releases negative.
Sunset salt tea light; breathing unfinished, finished, complete master teacher.

One cloud, one tree, cleanses one.
One cloud, glasses of gases.

Piano petal, flower petal, breeze petal pressed.
Piano petal, flower petal, the leather of leaf and the brass of sunlight.

Ringed finger trees, the ringing hand of leaves.
Ringed finger trees, the wind squeezes the leaves to clap.

Wooden white notes of day, black notes of night, piano fingertips of sun and moon.
Wooden white notes a breath seen, black notes a breath undone and unseen and undressed.

Runny music of spring's thawing wooden heart.
Runny music wind poured through thirsty trees into autumn glass, autumn grass, autumn ground.

Leaf wing, angle wing of piano plays prayer of the woods.
Leaf wing, angle wing angel.

Pegs of pine, pegs of violin voice, taught trees.
Pegs of pine, hand of air on the tightened trees.

Separate secretions of an all-metal autumn in suture, in sleep, in season.
Separate secretions of leaf on wind, of lip on breath, of light long rib in the woods.

Andrew G. Zubinas

Two clouds in the balcony, pine piano hand holds smile kiss.
Two clouds in the balcony, a cello of wood below, breathing sounds gray with sway and say.

Baton to bow breeze, violin length of leaves.
Baton to bow breeze, violin reflex of rustle.

Summer saturation of forest air.
Summer saturation of suppression.

The collected light, the collected digest of dawn and dusk.
The collected light, sun serpentine ore in the mines and mills of forest air.

Less impact, long or less autumn.
Less impact, less lung fall.

An inhaled fibrous fall, fall found in the digest.
An inhaled fibrous fall, autumn appreciable, air appreciable, appreciable also inhaled.

Lobe to lobe, leaf to leaf, season to season, site to site.
Lobe to lobe, the sampled scenes of seasons.

Ensemble of evening, melody and movement moon, melody and movement mirror mingle.
Ensemble of evening, evening engaging, forest wind rustle roams into romance.

Spring shorthand of thaw.
Spring shorthand breathing, summer long hand lung.

Rustle rhetoric reflection and reflex.
Rustle rhetoric shakes and spills pennies out of the bohemian breeze.

Breath lines, language lines of the bare trees, up and down writing with branching characters.
Breath lines, language lines latin across sunset horizon, latin across.

Regained baseline of sunrise, regained breathing.
Regained baseline of sunrise, the woods a weighted significance.

An ocean of wind, forest foam of the tree rings.
An ocean of wind, current coats of rings and uncoated bark.

Old winds; Lithuanian "senas" for old, rustle read of "ažuolas" for oak, and "beržas" for birch.
Old winds; forest senate, sentence, and senility of "klievas" for maple and "eglė" for pine tree.

Autumn audience applause; first violin of morning, second violin of afternoon, two violin voices.
Autumn audience applause; the viola of evening, the cello chest canopy unstrung by moonlight.

Teased-out trees, tea imbibed soil.
Teased-out trees, unclothed breathing of the wood, unclothed mind of the forest.

Old Scratch sky, length in, light in, the suture subdued, thunder tinnitus after.
Old Scratch sky, a branch in the sky, washed air of the forest.

Tree free, tree free breathing.
Tree free, tree freed from the fixed.

Entanglement of branches, branches of wind.
Entanglement of evening, helmet heat drop of the copper clad canopy fall.

Canopy color match, color mismatch; bury burn, burst burg autumn.
Canopy color match, lung match lit in the wind.

Low express leaf beginning to breathe.
Low express evening ending eye of moonlit forest.

Pine position of breathing.
Pine positioned over.

Roothold of gray, sprinkle and shower of leaf from cloud.
Roothold of gray, stem storm of wind.

Many minds and many moons of a honeycomb hive, the bone cement of honey.
Many minds and many moons of a honeycomb hive, the air cement of empty.

Andrew G. Zubinas

Art, Literature, and Religion:

Kremlin Gold: 1000 Years of Russian Gems. Harry N. Abrams, Inc., 100 Fifth Avenue, New York, N. Y. 10011. Internet www.abramsbooks.com. The State Museums of the Moscow Kremlin. The Houston Museum of Natural Science. The Field Museum. Hardcover. Exhibit book.

Land of the Winged Horsemen: Art in Poland 1572-1764. Copyright 1999 Art Services International, 700 North Fairfax Street, Suite 220, Alexandria, VA 22314. asi@clark.net www.artservicesintl.org Clothbound. Yale University Press. The Field Museum of Natural History Chicago, IL USA exhibit. Hardcover.

Minkevičius J. **Lietuvos Bažnyčių Menas The Art of Lithuanian Churches**. Copyright 1993. Vilnius. R. Paknio Leidykla. Hardcover.

Čiurlionis. Mikalojus Konstantinas Čiurlionis. 429 Reproductions. Copyright Leidykla "Vaga", 1977 Vilnius.

Čiurlionis, Mikalojus Konstantinas /1875-1911/. Simfoninės Poemos. Symphonic Poems. Miške (Forest) 18'22" Jūra (Sea) 36'56". Lietuvos Valstybinis Simfoninis Orkeststras Dirgentas Gintaras Rinkevičius. CD DDD copyright 2000. Vilniaus Plokštelių Studija/Semplice.

The Bible. Hardcover.

Shakespeare, William. **A Midsummer Night's Dream**. Audio recording.

Shakespeare, William. **As You Like It**. Audio recording.

How To Read and Understand Poetry. 24 Lectures. 12 Audio CDs. Taught by: Professor Willard Spigelman. Southern Methodist University. The Teaching Company. The Great Courses. Literature and English Language. Internet www.teach12.com.

The Lives and Works of the English Romantic Poets. 24 Lectures. 12 Audio CDs. Taught by: Professor Willard Spiegelman. Southern Methodist University. The Teaching Company. The Great Courses. Literature and English Language. Internet www.teach12.com.

124 Lithuanian books of poetry read out loud and dictated into a digital recorder

www.poetrysociety.org | poetry resources – publishers & journals.

www.google.com search word "definition" followed by a term

Piesarskas, Bronius. **DIDYSIS LIETUVIŲ-ANGLŲ KALBŲ ŽODYNAS** Apie 100 000 žodžių ir posakių. VILNIUS LEIDYKLA, ŽODYNAS" • 2006. Hardcover.

Medicine:

Tomashefski, Jr. et al. **Dail and Hammar's Pulmonary Pathology**. Volume I Nonneoplastic Lung Disease. Volume II Neoplastic Lung Disease. Springer Science + Business Media, LLC. Third Edition copyright 2008. Hardcover.

Bailey, Byron J. and Biller, Hugh F. **Surgery of the Larynx**. W. B. Saunders Company. Copyright 1986. West Washington Square, Philadelphia, PA 19105. Hardcover.

Fried, Marvin P. **The Larynx: A Multidisciplinary Approach**. Second Edition with 454 Illustrations. Mosby-Year Book, Inc. Copyright 1996. 11830 Westline Industrial Drive, St. Louis, Missouri 63146. Hardcover.

Ferlito, Alfio. **Diseases of the Larynx**. Oxford University Press Inc., 198 Madison Avenue, New York, NY 10016 Arnold, a member of the Hodder Headline Group, 338 Euston Road, London NW1 3BH http://www.arnoldpublishers.com copyright 2000. Hardcover.

Netter, Frank H. **The Netter Collection of Medical Illustrations Volume 7 Respiratory System**. A 13 volume set. Elsevier, Inc. Copyright 1980. Saunders Elsevier, 1660 John F. Kennedy Boulevard, Suite 1800, Philadelphia, Pennsylvania 19103-2899. Hardcover.

International Classification of Diseases 9th Revision Clinical Modification ICD-9-CM code set published by Ingenix. Spiral bound.

American Medical Association. **Current Procedural Terminology** CPT code set. Spiral bound.

DeVault K., Barta A, and Endicott M. **ICD-10-CM Coder Training Manual**. American Health Information Management Association (AHIMA), 233 North Michigan Avenue, 21st Floor, Chicago, IL 60601-5809. Copyright 2013. www.ahima.org

Campbell, Robert J. **Campbell's Psychiatric Dictionary**. Eighth edition. Oxford University Press. Copyright 2004. Oxford University Press, Inc., 198 Madison Avenue, New York, New York 10016. Internet http://www.oup.com Hardcover.

Sadock BJ, et al. **Kaplan & Sadock's Comprehensive Textbook of Psychiatry**. 2 Volumes. Copyright 2009. Wolters Kluwer | Lippincott Williams & Wilkins, 530 Walnut Street, Philadelphia, PA 19106 USA. Hardcover.

Pathology Board Review Course. 20 DVDs. The Oakstone Institute. Oakstone Medical Publishing, LLC. CME Continuing Medical Education. Web: www.cmeinfo. com.

Lambert, H. Wayne and Wineski, Lawrence E. **Lippincott's Illustrated Q & A Review of Anatomy and Embryology**. USMLE Step 1. United States Medical Licensing Exam Step 1. Copyright 2011. Lippincott Williams and Wilkins, a Wolters Kluwer business, 351 West Camden Street, Baltimore, MD 21201; Two Commerce Square, 2001 Market Street, Philadelphia, PA 19103 USA. Paperback.

West, John B. **Respiratory Physiology**. Copyright 1990. Williams & Wilkins, 429 East Preston Street, Baltimore, MD, 21202 USA. Paperback.

Cloutier, Michelle M. **Respiratory Physiology**. Copyright 2007 by Mosby, Inc., an affiliate of Elsevier Inc. Mosby Elsevier, 1600 John F. Kennedy Blvd., Ste 1800, Philadelphia, PA 19103-2899. Paperback. 217 pages.

Internet. Google term "Respiratory physiology PDF"

The New England Journal of Medicine. 2 weekly cases published under Images in Clinical Medicine. www.nejm.org

McDonough, Stefan I. **Calcium Channel Pharmacology**. Copyright 2004. Kluwer Academic / Plenum Publishers, New York. 233 Spring Street, New York, New York 10013. 418 pages. Hardcover.

Clinics in Chest Medicine: Pulmonary Arterial Hypertension. March 2007 Volume 28 Number 1. Guest Editor Harold I. Palevsky, MD. W.B. Saunders Company A division of Elsevier Inc. Elsevier Inc., 1600 John F. Kennedy Boulevard Suite 1800 Philadelphia, Pennsylvania 19103-2899. Hardcover.

Clinics in Chest Medicine: Pulmonary Manifestations of Rheumatic Disease. September 2010 Volume 31 Number 3. Guest Editor Kristin B Highland, MD, MSCR. W.B. Saunders Company

Otolaryngologic Clinics of North America: Meniere's Disease. Guest Editor Jeffrey P. Harris, MD, PhD Quyen T. Nguyen, MD, PhD October 2010 Volume 43 Number 5 W.B Saunders Company

STEDMAN'S MEDICAL DICTIONARY. 28th Edition Illustrated in Color. Copyright 2006. Lippincott Williams & Wilkins, A Wolters Kluwer Health Company, 351 West Camden Street, Baltimore, Maryland 21201-2436 USA www.stedmans.com stedmans@lww.com Hardcover.

MOSBY'S MEDICAL DICTIONARY 8th Edtion Illustrated in full color throughout With over 2450 illustrations. MOSBY ELSEVIER. 11830 Westline Industrial Drive, St. Louis, Missouri 63146. Hardcover. Copyright 2009.

DORLAND'S ILLUSTRATED MEDICAL DICTIONARY 32nd EDITION DELUXE. ELSEVIER SAUDERS 1600 John F. Kennedy Blvd, Ste 1800, Philadelphia, PA 19103-2899. Copyright 2102. Hardcover.

American Psychological Association. **APA Dictionary of Psychology**. Gary R. VandenBos, PhD Editor in Chief. Copyright 2007. American Psychological Association, 750 First Street, NE, Washington, DC 2002. www.apa.org Hardcover.

Otolaryngologic Clinics series

Anesthesia Clinics series

Sleep Medicine Clinics

Secret series in Medicine

Glasscock III, Michael E. Gulya, Aina Juliana. **Glasscock-Shambaugh Surgery of the Ear**. Copyright 2003 BC Decker Inc., United States, BC Decker Inc, P.O. Box 785, Lewsiton, NY 14092-0785 Tel: 905-522-7017; 800-568-7281 Fax: 905-522-7839; 888-311-4987 E-mail: info@dcdecker.com www.bcdecker.com Hardcover. 808 pages.

Katz, J. et al. **Handbook of Clinical Audiology** Sixth Edition Copyright 2009 Lippincott Williams and Wilkins, 351 West Camden Street, Baltimore, Maryland 21201-2436 USA, 227 East Washington Square, Philadelphia, PA 19106 internet http://www.lww.com Hardcover. 1032 pages.

Brckmann et al. **Otologic Surgery**. W.B. Saunders Company A Division of Harcourt Brace & Company. The Curtis Center. Independence Square West. Philadelphia, Pennsylvania 19106. Copyright 1994. Hardcover 802 pages.

Wiener Stanley L. **Differential Diagnosis of Acute Pain By Body Region**. Stanley L. Wiener, M.D. Professor of Medicine Formerly, Chief, Section of General Internal Medicine The University of Illinois College of Medicine Chicago Chicago, Illinois. McGraw-Hill, Inc. Copyright 1993. During my Introduction to Clinical Medicine course, this professor of mine (I think his rank was colonel in the United States military) used to brandish his middle finger at me during his lectures in a gesture of contempt day after day, lecture after lecture. The man's eye was deviated to one side – a real disorder of the globe. That was before the grades of

Micro U, Pharm S, Psychopath S, and Micro S, Pharm U, Psychopath U. That was before stepping out of the United States Medical licensing exam step 1 and witnessing a doctor getting a bought of whiplash. That was before my reapplication to professional school myself being given a bought of whiplash with my car totaled (on my way to the library of course).

Natural Science, Natural History, & Nature:

Sanders, Jack. **The Secrets of Wildflowers**. Copyright 2003. The Lyons Press is an imprint of The Globe Pequot Press. The Field Museum of Natural History online bookstore in Chicago. Hardcover.

Ubick, D., P. Paquin, P.E. Cushing, and V. Roth (eds). 2005. **Spiders of North America: an identification manual**. American Arachnological Society, Keene (New

Hampshire). 377 pages. The American Museum of Natural History online bookstore in New York. Spiral bound.

Gray, Theodore. **The Elements: A Visual Exploration of Every Known Atom in the Universe**. Copyright 2009. Black Dog & Leventhal Publishers, Inc., 151 West 19th Street, New York, NY 10011. The American Museum of Natural History online bookstore in New York. Hardcover.

Nicklin, Charles "Flip." **Among Giants: A Life with Whales**. Copyright 2011 by Paraculture, Inc. www.paraculture.com The University of Chicago Press. The American Museum of Natural History online bookstore in New York. Hardcover.

Mikkelsen et al., **Seashells of Southern Florida**. Copyright 2008. Princeton University Press, 41 William Street, Princeton, New Jersey 08540. The Field Museum of Natural History in Chicago online bookstore. Hardcover.

Cassie B. et al. **A World of Butterflies**. Copyright 2004 by Chanticleer Press, Inc. Bulfinch Press. Hachette Book Group, 237 Park Avenue, New York, NY 10017. Hatchettebookgroup.com The Smithsonian Institute online bookstore. Hardcover.

The Great Courses. www.teach12.com **Great Ideas of Classical Physics**. 24 Lectures. DVDs. Taught by: Professor Steven Pollock. University of Colorado at Boulder. Science & Mathematics. THE TEACHING COMPANY. 4840 Westfields Boulevard, Suite 500, Chantilly, Virginia 20151-2299. 1-800-TEACH-12 Fax-703-378-3819 www.teach12.com Copyright The Teaching Company, 2006.

The Great Courses. www.teach12.com **Quantum Mechanics: The Physics of the Microscopic World**. 24 Lectures. DVDs. Taught by: Professor Benjamin Schumacher. Kenyon College. Science & Mathematics. THE TEACHING COMPANY. 4840 Westfields Boulevard, Suite 500, Chantilly, Virginia 20151-2299 1-800-TEACH-12 Fax-703-378-3819 www.teach12.com Copyright The Teaching Company, 2009.

The Great Courses. www.teach12.com **Physics and Our Universe: How It All Works**.

60 Lectures. DVDs. Professor Richard Wolfson. Middlebury College. Science & Mathematics. THE GREAT COURSES. Corporate Headquarters. 4840 Westfields Boulevard, Suite 500, Chantilly, Virginia 20151-2299 Phone: 1-800-832-2412 Fax: 703-378-3819 www.thegreatcourses.com Copyright The Teaching Company 2011.

Kinsler et al. **Fundamentals of Acoustics**. Hardcover.

Kelley, Mark. **Alaska: A Photographic Excursion**. Southeast Alaska, Prince William Sound, Denali National Park. Printed by Samhwa Printing Co., Ltd., Seoul, Korea through Alaska Print Brokers, Anchorage, Alaska. Mark Kelley can be reached at PO Box 20470, Juneau, AK 99802; by phone: toll free number (888) 933-1993 or (907)586-1993; by FAX: (907) 586-1201; or by email: photos@markkelley.com; Web site: www.markkelley.com. Photographs by Mark Kelley. Narration by Nick Jans. Copyright 2007. Carnival Cruise Ship gift shop. Hardcover.

Kelley, Mark. **Alaska's Tracy Arm Fords Terror Wilderness**. Featuring Dawes and Sawyer Glaciers. Photos by Mark Kelly. Written by Nick Jans. Copyright 2012 by Mark Kelley. Carnival Cruise Ship gift shop. Hardcover.

Kelley, Mark et al. **Alaska's Watchable Whales Humpback and Killer Whales**. The Six Alaskans who worked on this book – three photographers and three writers: Mark Kelley, Jay Beedle, Jayleen Beedle, Linda Daniel, Scott Foster, Nick Jans. Copyright 2011. Carnival Cruise Ship gift shop. Hardcover.

Wikipedia: a list of botanical gardens and arboretums in the United States of America.

Journals that I subscribe to:

The New England Journal of Medicine

Journal of Voice (Official Journal of the Voice Foundation and the International Association of Phonosurgery)(www.jvoice.org)

Journal of the Acoustical Society of America

Journals at the Office:

CPSIA information can be obtained
at www.ICGtesting.com
Printed in the USA
LVOW03s1705180117

521406LV00001B/3/P